"I need a description of your dresses for the newspaper article," Pamela explained. "Could I see one of them?"

Sunshine could see the eyes of the other girls get big.

"The dresses aren't here," Ducky said smoothly. "Can we show them to you in a few days?"

"They're going to be a surprise," Carlie said.

That was no lie!

"Okay," Pamela said. "Let me know as soon as you can."

Sunshine walked to the door with Pamela and Jeff, but when she opened it, she saw Arvy and Jamahl on the porch. Arvy's arms were piled high with something yellow and feathery. Chicken suits from the Buck-a-Cluck Chicken Shack. Jamahl carried an enormous bag from which a big chicken foot protruded.

Sunshine stared at them.

"We brought your bridesmaids' outfits," Arvy said. "You asked how many chicken outfits there were, and I said six. You said you needed six bridesmaids' outfits, and I said I'd see if the suits were available."

"I *didn't* say I wanted them for bridesmaids' outfits," Sunshine said. "I just meant . . ."

THE
BRIDESMAIDS'
DRESS
DISASTER

THE BRIDESMAIDS' DRESS DISASTER

LAEL LITTKE

Published by
Deseret Book Company
Salt Lake City, Utah

Library of Congress Cataloging-in-Publication Data

Littke, Lael.
     The bridesmaids' dress disaster / Lael Littke.
        p.   cm. — (Bee Theres ; bk. 5)
     "Cinnamon Tree."
     Summary: When the former teacher of her Beehive church group plans to be married, twelve-year-old Sunshine faces serious problems as she tries to come up with a design for bridesmaid dresses for herself and six other friends.
     ISBN 0–87579–940–X
     [1. Mormons—Fiction. 2. Weddings—Fiction.] I. Title.
II. Series: Littke, Lael. Bee Theres ; bk. 5.
PZ7.L719Br   1994
[Fic]—dc20   94–30487
                                            CIP
                                            AC

Printed in the United States of America

10 9 8 7 6 5 4 3 2 1

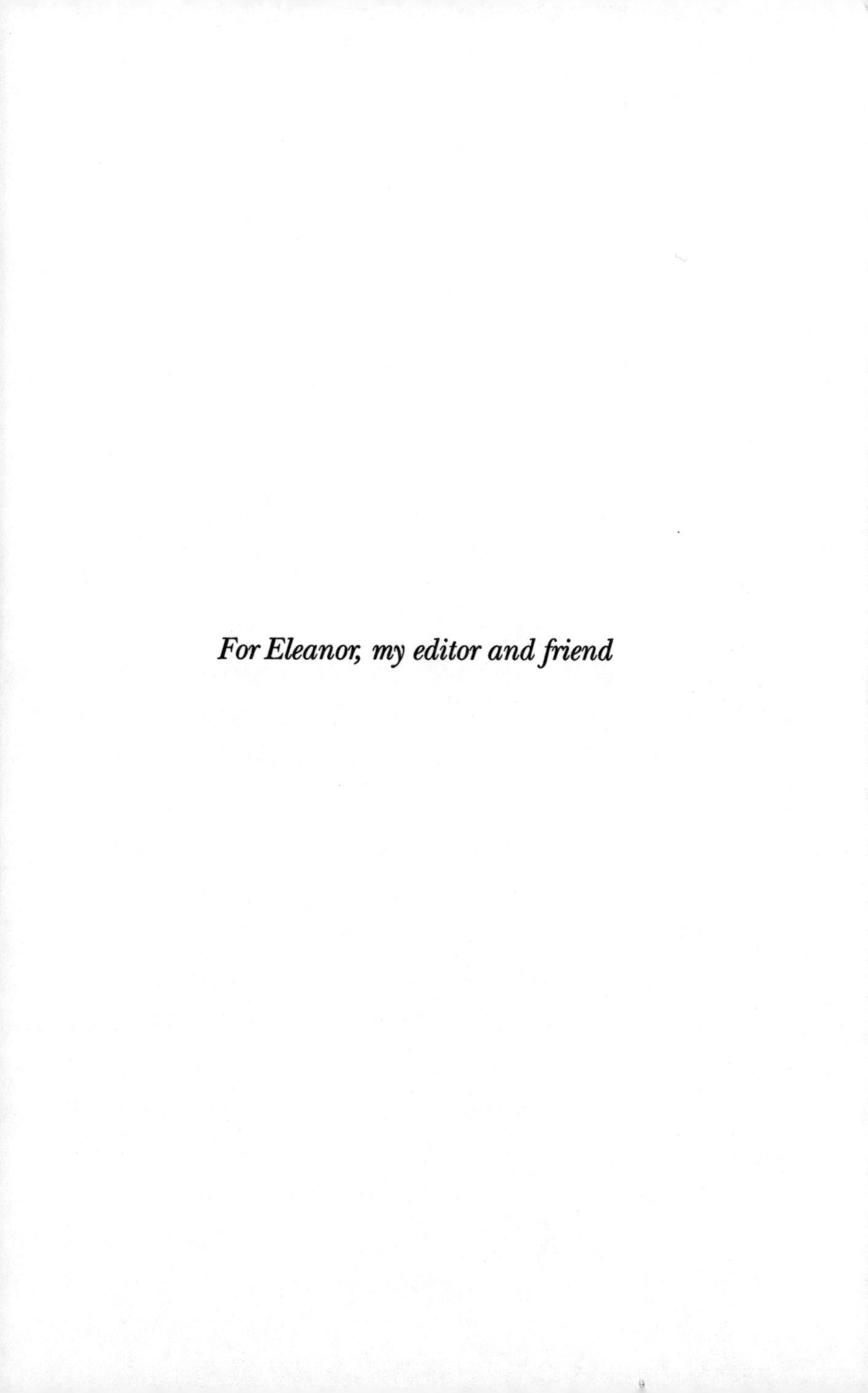

For Eleanor, my editor and friend

CHAPTER 1

Sunshine was trying on names.

"Berta," she said softly. "Marlis. Phoebe."

Peering at herself in her small bedroom mirror, she tried to determine whether she was a Berta, a Marlis, or a Phoebe.

None of them seemed quite right.

One thing she wasn't was a Sunshine. That had been a good enough name when she was a little kid. But now that she was twelve and was going to be a bridesmaid at a wedding reception, she needed a name that didn't sound so babyish. Something that was still distinctive and different but that would look good in the newspaper announcement along with the names of the other girls in her Beehive class.

They were all going to be bridesmaids for Pamela,

who was their Beehive teacher before she went home to Idaho to get ready for her wedding.

"Bridesmaids," the newspaper announcement would say, "were Carlie Kuramoto, Becca Martin, Elena Perez, Marybeth Stewart, and . . . " And *Sunshine* McGee?

Sunshine sighed. It was all her mother's fault. Why hadn't she named her something elegant like Cordelia, or Nicolette, or maybe Guinevere, the name of the queen in the show *Camelot* that the high school had put on last spring? Her mother, who taught at the high school, had taken Sunshine to see it. She'd even commented about how much she liked the name Guinevere. Why hadn't she thought of that twelve years ago?

The phone rang out in the hall. Sunshine didn't have a phone in her room as most of her friends did. She and her mom got along with one phone, one TV, one car. They also had one old dog named Brunhilda who always seemed to curl up and sleep right where people needed to walk. Sunshine had to step over her to get to the phone table.

Their phone was old, bright yellow, and wasn't even a Touch-Tone like everybody else's. It had a dial. Her mother had bought it at a garage sale.

"Hello," Sunshine said as she picked it up.

"Guess what?"

Sunshine knew it was Becca calling. Becca was like that. She expected everybody to know who she was after only two words. And she was always springing stuff like "Guess what," or "You'll never believe," or "You'll just die when I tell you."

"Hi, Becca," Sunshine said. "I can't guess."

"You'll just die when I tell you," Becca said.

"Well, wait till I lie down then," Sunshine said. "I don't want to hurt myself when I fall over to die."

"Sunshine." Becca's voice lowered a couple of notches as if what she was going to say was bad news.

Sunshine tightened her grip on the telephone. What could have happened?

"There's going to be a new girl in our Beehive class," Becca announced.

A new girl? Sunshine waited to hear what was so bad about that. A new girl in the class could be fun.

The phone line hummed. Sunshine knew Becca expected her to say something, so she repeated, "A new girl."

Becca moaned. "Yes. You'll never believe her name."

Probably it was one of the pretty names that were popular right now, like Britny, or Cady, or maybe Chelsea.

If it wasn't, maybe Sunshine would pick one of those for herself. Cady would be nice. That was different but sounded like the nineties. "Cady McGee" would look terrific in the newspaper announcement.

"What *is* her name?" Sunshine asked.

"It's Ducky Dumont."

Becca was right. Sunshine didn't believe it. Nobody would name a child "Ducky."

"It's true," Becca insisted. "Sister Jackson told me herself."

Sister Jackson had been their Beehive teacher since Pamela left. Sunshine knew she would never say anything that wasn't true. Sister Jackson wasn't just striving for perfection; she was already there. But then she'd had plenty of time to *get* perfect, since she was about as old as Noah.

"Ducky." Sunshine tried saying the name. She liked the girl already. Anybody who'd suffered through that name for twelve years deserved to be liked.

"Yes." Becca groaned again. "Isn't it the pits?"

"It's no worse than Sunshine." Sunshine didn't realize she'd said it aloud until Becca said, "I didn't mean the name, which is bad enough. But it's the pits that we have to have a new girl in the class right now when we're getting ready for Pamela's wedding. Will she want to be a bridesmaid, too? Maybe Sister Jackson won't let us talk about the wedding in class if Ducky isn't included." Becca stopped to take a breath, then went on. "Maybe Pamela will even uninvite us to be bridesmaids so we won't hurt Ducky's feelings."

Pamela had been such a great Beehive teacher. She was beautiful, with a glamorous job as an airline attendant. She'd done terrific things, like teach the girls how to apply makeup, and she'd taken them mall-shopping, and they'd had sleep-overs at her apartment.

Ducky had missed all that. Maybe Pamela *would* think it would be too mean for them all to be bridesmaids and leave Ducky out.

"We can talk about the wedding at our Bee Theres meetings," Sunshine suggested. "Maybe Ducky won't even have to know about it."

The Bee Theres was a club Sunshine and the other class members had started when they'd first become Beehive girls. They'd made a vow that they would always "Be There" for one another. Their favorite place to have meetings was at McDonald's, where they could munch burgers and fries while they discussed whatever was going on at the moment.

"What if Ducky wants to be a Bee There?" Becca said.

"Maybe we'll want her to be." Sunshine wasn't too sure she'd want a stranger in their club, but on the other hand, this poor Ducky person was going to need friends.

"What if all the guys like her?" Becca said this as if that would be the greatest trial of all.

What guys? The Scouts? Dale Delancy and Arvy Dixon and the others? Every time those grungy Scouts saw Sunshine and her friends, they chanted, "Buzzy, buzzy Beehives, looking for their honey." Who cared if all of them buzzed over to Ducky?

Of course, there was also Gregory Okinaga, who wasn't a Mormon but who came to church and Scout meetings all the time because he liked Carlie.

And Marybeth liked Sam Adkins, who'd recently moved there to Pasadena to live with his brother Quincy.

Elena sort of liked Augie Krump. When the Bee Theres had last played the Guy Game, it had come out that she was supposed to have her first date with him when she turned sixteen.

Becca wrote to a guy named Joshua, whom the Bee Theres had met when they spent a week at an old historical farm in Utah. Ducky wasn't likely to even meet him.

As for Sunshine, she didn't like any guy in partic-ular. What guy would want a girl with a baby name like Sunshine? Sunshine suspected that Ducky had the same problem.

Her hand was getting cramped, and she shifted the phone to the other one. "Why don't we just welcome her to our class on Sunday and see what happens? Maybe we'll like her a lot."

"Okay." Becca sounded cheerful now that she'd laid all her worries on Sunshine. "Sister Jackson said she'll add a whole new dimension to our class, whatever that means."

They said good-bye at the same time that Brunhilda woke up and started to bark. She always barked when anybody came near their house. This time it was a happy bark, which meant Sunshine's mother had arrived home.

She came through the back door, dumping her armload of books on the hall table she'd made from a plank (painted yellow) and a couple of old orange crates (painted orange). She patted Brunhilda, who'd come in with her, then said, "Hi, Sunny. What's happening?"

"We're getting a new girl in our Beehive class," Sunshine said. "Her name's Ducky."

"I love it," Mom said.

Sunshine had figured she would. Mom wasn't like the mothers of the other Bee Theres. She dressed in tie-dyed T-shirts and long, swirly skirts and sandals she found at garage sales. On Mom these things looked good. She wore ear-cuffs and big, jangly bracelets, and sometimes funky little velvet hats over her long, straight, blonde hair that was so much like Sunshine's. Mom liked to be different.

So did Sunshine. She wore the same kind of clothes as her mom, and she took pride in being different from the other girls. It was the one thing that really set her apart and gave her a separate identity.

The only thing she *didn't* like was her name. Sunshine. It was too silly for a newspaper announcement about a wedding.

"Mom," she said, "do I look like a Margaret? Or maybe a Tallulah?"

Mom had opened the refrigerator door and was peering inside, probably to see if any lentil soup was left from yesterday or if she'd have to prepare something else. "Margaret would be fine if you're going to be our first woman president," she said. "If you're hoping to be a great actress, Tallulah would be just right."

She closed the refrigerator door. Apparently the lentil soup was all gone, which didn't make Sunshine too unhappy. But that meant they'd have alfalfa-sprout salad or something equally yucky for dinner. Mom liked weird food and *never* suggested that they should go out and have something really good like Big Macs and fries.

Turning to look at Sunshine, Mom said, "What's

all this about names? Are you planning to change yours?"

"Maybe." Sunshine knew Mom wouldn't object. She was named Lucinda after her grandmother, but she'd told Sunshine that before she was married she'd called herself Breeze.

Sunshine wondered if Ducky was the new girl's real name. Maybe she was little and cute and blonde, a cheerleader type, like Fuffy Richards or Bunny Tambo at school.

Sunshine could hardly wait to meet her on Sunday.

When Sunday came, Sunshine put on her white dress and white shoes, with a sunflower barrette holding back her hair. It wasn't the way she usually dressed, but she didn't want to startle this Ducky Dumont on her first time in the Beehive class.

Now if only she could decide on her new name so that Ducky would never have to know about "Sunshine." But maybe having somebody else with a goofy first name would make Ducky feel more at home.

Nevertheless, she had to pick her new name soon, because the wedding was only a few weeks off, and the announcement would have to be ready to put in the newspaper right afterward.

Beatrice, maybe?

She didn't look like a Beatrice.

"Come on," her mother called. "Let's go."

She thought of other names during sacrament meeting. Alicia? Gwendolyn? Maybe something foreign and exotic-sounding, like Solange? After all, hadn't one of her great-grandmothers come from France? Wasn't that where Sunshine had gotten her sense of style and her talent for designing dresses, which was something she liked to do?

The other Beehives kept turning their heads around, probably looking for someone new who looked like a Ducky. But everybody in the chapel wore familiar faces. So where was Ducky? Sunshine filed away the names she'd been thinking about to consider later. She watched for Ducky, too.

But Ducky didn't come.

She wasn't in their Sunday School class either. There were only the five girls plus the Scouts, who sat on the back row in the classroom. They did gross things like make armpit music, until Brother Nordstrom got them involved in writing stuff on the chalkboard and passing out a questionnaire about the lesson.

By the time their Beehive class started, the girls had decided Ducky Dumont wasn't coming. Even

Sister Jackson looked anxiously out the window of the upstairs room where their class met.

"Maybe she's too shy to come," Sunshine said. "Maybe we should go to her house after class and welcome her to our ward."

Sister Jackson nodded. "That's very thoughtful of you, Sunshine. We'll do that if she doesn't come. Now, let's have the opening prayer and get on with our lesson for today. Marybeth?"

Marybeth was their Beehive class president. She called on Sunshine to pray.

Sunshine stood up, folded her arms, closed her eyes, and tried to think of what to say besides the usual things about blessing Sister Jackson that she'd give a good lesson and all the girls that they would listen and apply the lesson to their lives. "Bless Ducky Dumont," she said, then couldn't think of what she should be blessed with. Finally she said, "Bless Ducky Dumont that she might come to our class."

She'd no sooner said "Amen" than the door banged open and a girl zinged into the room, the most beautiful girl Sunshine had ever seen.

"Hey, dudettes," the girl sang out. "I'm here!" She flung her arms out as if she were on a stage, the same way the whole cast did in the finale of the roadshow they'd done that summer.

She was taller than Sunshine and just as thin, but

her thinness was shaped, not just straight up and down. She had black hair done up in what seemed like a thousand cornrows with bright beads on the ends. She wore an outfit that was red and purple and blue, something that looked so good with her caramel skin that it was an absolute treat just to let your eyes rest on her.

Sunshine had seen a movie once called *The African Queen.* That's what Ducky looked like. An African Queen. It had been the name of a boat in the movie, but that's what Sunshine thought of, anyway.

Nobody said a thing. They all stared silently at Ducky. She didn't seem to notice. Floating over to a chair and wafting gracefully down onto it, she said, "Hey, I'm sorry I'm late. I was on a shoot. It won't happen again." She flashed a white-toothed smile that lit up the room.

Still nobody said anything.

"I'm Ducky Dumont," the girl said.

Sunshine's heart sank. In one split second Ducky Dumont had totally scuttled her only claim to fame—being the "different" one among the young women of the ward.

She had a feeling that the Beehive class—and her life—would never again be the same.

CHAPTER 2

Sister Jackson spoke before any of the girls found their voices.

"We're delighted to have you in our class, Ducky," she said. "And since you've been so kind as to introduce yourself, we'll all do the same. I'm Sister Rhoda Jackson, the Beehive leader." She smiled at Ducky, then looked at the class. "You be next, Becca."

Becca hesitated a moment, as if she couldn't remember her name. She kept staring at Ducky, not even blinking. Finally she said, "I'm Becca Martin."

"Hey, I'm glad to meet you," Ducky said.

As the other girls said their names, Ducky flashed that brilliant smile of hers and told them how glad she was to know them. She seemed to mean it, too.

If Ducky hadn't been so totally gorgeous, so exotic, so *different* from anybody else Sunshine had ever known, she probably would have liked her immediately. But Sunshine just couldn't get around that *different* part. She, Sunshine, was supposed to be the different one. She was used to being known for her weird clothes and strange tastes and sometimes outrageous behavior. And here was this Ducky Dumont, moving right into her territory and taking it over.

Sunshine felt pale and washed out and colorless beside Ducky. In her white dress, she was suddenly a tapioca pudding sitting next to a triple-decker death-by-chocolate spice cake like the one her mom made occasionally when she wanted to wow somebody.

Well, Sunshine wasn't going to give up her place in the world without a fight.

But hadn't Ducky said something about having been out shooting that morning? Did she carry a gun? Was she dangerous?

Sunshine raised her hand. "What were you shooting?" she asked, looking straight at Ducky.

"Commercials," Ducky said.

Carlie leaped to her feet. "I've seen you," she said. "On TV. On that commercial where you're feeding a tiger."

Sunshine had seen that too. And here was the very girl who'd been in it, right here in their Beehive class.

Ducky nodded. "I'm sorry I'm late," she said again. "Did I miss the lesson?"

"No, we're just ready for it now," Sister Jackson said. "If we finish in time, we'll talk about what needs to be done for the wedding."

Ducky's eyes widened. "Is one of you getting married?"

Everybody, even Sunshine, laughed because Ducky looked so startled.

"Well, look," Ducky said. "I haven't been a Mormon for very long. For all I know, you might believe in getting married when you're twelve."

Grinning, Carlie said, "It's Pamela who's getting married. She's twenty-six. She was our Beehive teacher before Sister Jackson. We're all going to be bridesmaids."

"Bridesmaids!" Ducky exclaimed. "Well, hey, if you need a fashion consultant, just ask me."

Sunshine felt her ears get hot. *She* was the one who was going to do the bridesmaids' dresses. Pamela knew how much she liked to sew and how she wanted to design dresses when she got older. Since the bridesmaids were just going to be circulating around with plates of hors d'oeuvres and things like that, Pamela said it didn't really matter if their dresses matched the maid-of-honor's dress, so she'd asked Sunshine to design something the girls would like.

She'd also asked the girls what color dresses they wanted to wear, and after they'd decided on peach, she'd sent some gorgeous polished-cotton print material, creamy background with peach and orange and pale yellow flowers all over. Sunshine was going to make the dresses from this material, as soon as she decided on a design.

Now Ducky was trying to get into the act.

"Girls," Sister Jackson interrupted, "let's get to our lesson. We'll try to leave time to talk at the end of the class."

Sunshine scarcely heard the lesson. The subject was family history. She couldn't keep her mind on it because she was thinking about how she could reclaim her life as it had been before Ducky Dumont had appeared ten minutes ago and totally messed it up.

"On our next activity night," Sister Jackson said at the end of the lesson, "we're going to have a grandmothers party. I want each of you to pick one of your female ancestors and be her for the evening. Dress as much like her as you can. Make something from one of her recipes. Bring pictures. If you happen to have her journal, bring that too, or anything else that belonged to her."

Marybeth put her hand up. Without waiting to be called on, she said, "My great-great-great-grandmother came across the plains in a handcart company. We've got one of her dresses. I'll wear it."

Sunshine knew Marybeth was very proud of her pioneer ancestors.

"My great-great-grandmother was a suffragette," Becca announced. "I'll bring some of the things she wrote."

Sunshine remembered a report Becca had made on her great-great-grandmother for a social studies class at school. She had organized marches and had given speeches about passing an amendment to the U.S. Constitution so that women could vote.

"My great-great-grandmother was a slave," Ducky said softly. "She got away to the North on the Underground Railway and then helped other slaves to escape too. I can tell one of the stories she passed down to us."

Nobody said anything after that. Ducky had topped them all. Smiling, Sister Jackson said, "See what an exciting grandmothers night we're going to have? Learn all you can about the ancestor you pick and tell us about her that night." She cleared her throat. "Now, we have a few minutes to talk. Ducky, why don't you tell us how you came to join the Church."

Ducky grinned. "You know what? It was because of a roadshow. My friend Tami, where I used to live, was a Mormon, and she invited me to come be in their roadshow. They let me sing two solos, and I had so much fun with all the kids and liked them so much that I asked the missionaries to teach me, and here I am!"

Sunshine glanced at Elena, who was watching Ducky with a thoughtful look on her face. Elena had wanted more than anything to be star of the roadshow they'd put on six weeks ago. Even though she was the best singer in the ward, she hadn't got the starring role, which had gone to an older girl. The leaders had said Elena was young and would be in other shows.

Now here was Ducky, already prepared to be the star of the next show.

Sunshine could see that Elena was feeling about the same way she was, that this new Ducky person was moving in and camping on space that was already claimed.

Ducky didn't seem to notice anything was wrong. She was telling about her family. "My brother, Anton, joined the Church too. He's seventeen. My mom isn't a member, but my dad was baptized just before we moved here. You'll all get acquainted with him. He's the new principal of the junior high where we'll be going." She looked around. "At least I guess we'll all be going there. The one a few blocks south of the church?"

The other girls nodded.

Sunshine glanced at Marybeth, who was hoping to be a class officer when they started junior high. Would Ducky take over there too?

It was time for an emergency Bee Theres meeting at McDonald's. They needed to talk about the coming wedding, but she was sure the main subject of discussion would be Ducky Dumont.

"Our time is gone," Sister Jackson said. "We didn't get around to talking about the wedding today, so we'll do it next Sunday. There's still time." She closed her lesson book. "We'll have the closing prayer, then we'll be dismissed."

Ducky put up her hand. "I'll give it," she said.

Didn't she know that you didn't just volunteer to do things like that?

After class, Ducky ran on ahead, saying she had to make a phone call. "I have to tell them I can't shoot on Sundays anymore," she said. "They'll have to change to Saturdays because I want to be here on Sundays."

She disappeared down the stairs, leaving the Bee Theres whispering together.

Carlie was the only one who didn't think they

needed an emergency Bee Theres meeting to discuss Ducky Dumont.

"I think she's terrific," Carlie said. "I've never met anybody quite like her before. It's going to be fun having her with us."

"Well, I like her too," Sunshine said, not quite sure it was true. "But we can't just let her take over *everything* we've been doing."

"She's not taking over *everything*," Carlie argued.

Up ahead they could see Ducky standing at the pay phone in the foyer.

As they watched, Dale Delancy and Arvy Dixon and the other Scouts came dashing through, probably on their way to horse around outside.

The boys skidded to a stop when they saw Ducky. Dale poked Arvy and said something to him. Augie Krump stopped dead in his tracks and stared. Gregory Okinaga almost strolled right on by, but then he saw Ducky too. He stopped. He straightened his tie. He licked his hand and ran it back over his already neat hair.

The guys all stood there until Ducky finished her phone call. When she turned around and saw them, she flashed that megawatt smile of hers. "Hi," she said.

Dale and Arvy suddenly started to punch each other's arms and fall over their own feet.

Augie collapsed on one of the foyer chairs.

Gregory smiled back at Ducky and said, "Hi. I'm Greg."

On the stairway Carlie watched. Then she turned to the other Bee Theres. "When is it you want to have that emergency Bee Theres meeting?"

They set the meeting at McDonald's for the next day, Monday, at noon. This was the last week they'd be able to meet at noon, since school would be starting the following week.

When Sunshine got home, she went straight to her bedroom and stared at herself in her mirror.

"Mirror, mirror, on the wall," she said, "who is fairest of us all?"

She knew what the mirror would say if it could talk.

And with a name like Ducky, too!

Sunshine remembered that before Ducky had come into her life, she'd been trying to pick a new name for herself. Something that would look good in the newspaper announcement about Pamela's wedding. Something that would have more pizzazz than Sunshine.

Arabella, maybe? Hillary?

She needed more than a new name now.

She needed a new personality. A new body. A new look.

She picked up a handful of her pale blonde hair and looked at it. *Totally* tapioca pudding.

She could begin the remake of herself by dyeing her hair.

"Mom," she called, running into the kitchen where her mother sat at the dark green table she'd picked up along the street on a super-trash day and had refinished and painted. It looked good with the fake Bentwood chairs she'd bought at Cost Plus.

Her mother looked up from the literature book she was reading in preparation for classes she would be teaching next week. "Where's the fire?"

"Mom," Sunshine said. "I'm going to dye my hair."

"What color?"

Her mom never objected to anything Sunshine wanted to do. Sometimes Sunshine wished she would. She almost wished now that she would say, "Why would you want to color your beautiful hair? It's so pretty just as it is."

But she didn't say that.

What color? Sunshine wasn't sure. Red, maybe? But it might turn out to be a shade that wouldn't look good with the colors of the bridesmaids' dresses for Pamela's wedding.

She was already blonde, so that was out.

Brown? Not spectacular enough.

Black? No. Ducky's hair was black, and Sunshine didn't want anybody to think she was copying her.

Suddenly she knew.

"Purple," she said. "I'm going to dye my hair purple."

Let Ducky Dumont try to top that!

CHAPTER
3

Sunshine's mom didn't even blink when Sunshine announced she was going to dye her hair purple. All she said was, "When do you want to do it?"

Sunshine thought about it. She'd better do it right away before she lost her courage. "Tomorrow morning," she said. "As soon as the drugstore opens and I can get the dye."

"Okay." Mom went back to the book she was reading.

So it was all set.

Sunshine went to her room to draw sketches of the bridesmaids' dresses. She wanted to get something on paper before Ducky Dumont started coming up with designs.

Brunhilda followed her, curling up by her chair. Sunshine patted her. Mom had used more imagination in naming the dog than she had in choosing a name for *her*. Maybe she should change *her* name to Brunhilda.

The next morning after Sunshine had picked up the dye from the drugstore, she suddenly wasn't as eager to dye her hair purple as she'd been the day before. Her hair was all right as it was, wasn't it? Long and straight and pale. She'd always liked her hair.

But then she thought of Ducky and her vivid coloring.

"Mom," she said, "maybe I'll dye just part of my hair." She picked up a long handful of hair that grew from the crown of her head and fell down her back. "If I dye this, I can just let it blend in with the rest of my hair or I can wear it in a long purple braid."

Mom looked up from the table where she was reading the *Los Angeles Times* and crunching a bowl of cereal. She cupped her hand under her chin as she looked at Sunshine.

"Hmmmm," she said. "You know what? I'd like it better if you did a lock that hangs down to the right, over your cheek. Then it would contrast with your skin tones and show up from the front."

She got to her feet and picked up some hair from the center of Sunshine's head. Quickly she braided it. "Now imagine this being purple."

Sunshine liked it. "How can we do just that piece without getting purple on everything else?"

"Easy." Mom got out an old shower cap and told Sunshine to put it over her hair. Then she cut a hole and pulled through it the thick lock that was to be purple.

"Time to apply the dye," she said, opening the bottle Sunshine had bought at the drugstore.

Sunshine had a bad moment as Mom smeared on the goopy dye. It smelled strong, and it looked black when it was on her hair. Was this going to be a total disaster? She'd read the book *Anne of Green Gables* when she was younger. She'd laughed when Anne tried to dye her red hair black, only to have it turn out green. What if *her* hair turned green? Would it matter? She'd seen kids at school with green hair, and pink, too, and orange. Whatever came out would be okay.

It didn't take long. After Mom got the dye put on, Sunshine sat and read part of the *Times* while she waited for it to take. She liked to read the funnies and Dear Abby's column. Today Dear Abby had a letter from a girl who complained that her sister read her diary.

Sunshine wondered if she should write to Dear Abby about Ducky Dumont. "Dear Abby," she'd say, "There's this girl who just moved into our ward." No, she couldn't say that. Dear Abby probably wouldn't know what a ward was.

"Dear Abby," she'd say, "There's this new girl. She's gorgeous. She's even got a shape and probably wears a bra."

Was that what really bothered her about Ducky?

Well, yes, but not the major thing.

"Dear Abby," she'd have to say, "The only way I'm different from everybody else is that I'm different. But now there's a new girl who is a *different* different from me, and I'm green with jealousy."

That wouldn't do either. But speaking of green, it was probably time to look at her hair.

It turned out perfect, not wishy-washy lavender but not so dark that it looked black. It was definitely purple, a warm, bright purple that looked neat with her peachy skin.

So what else could she do to out-different Ducky Dumont? Dangly purple earrings? A purple nose jewel?

How about a nose *ring*?

Sunshine wasn't sure how her mom would feel about that. It'd probably be all right with her mom if she had her ears pierced, but nose piercing was another thing.

She decided against it, unless Ducky should suddenly appear with a nose ring. Then she'd be mad that she hadn't been the first one to do it.

Sighing, she got dressed. She put on a bright purple camp shirt she had found at a thrift shop for a dollar. There'd been a big dark spot on the front that wouldn't come out, but Mom had embroidered around and through it so that now it looked as if it was supposed to be there. One of Mom's gauzy skirts was still there in her closet from the last time Sunshine had worn it. It was full of soft shades of purple, orange, and green. She put it on, letting the shirt hang down over it. Next, she pulled on the black combat boots she and Mom had found in an army surplus store. Last of all, she attached a dragon ear-cuff to the edge of her left ear.

She looked at herself in her mirror. The shirt was too big and bagged down off her shoulders. The skirt was long, hanging down almost to the tops of her boots, and its hem was uneven. Her two-tone hair looked a little tangled, as if she'd just got up and hadn't yet combed it.

Perfect. She looked just right.

She shoved the sketches of the bridesmaids' dresses she'd drawn last night into a big envelope and left the house.

The other Bee Theres were already at McDonald's when she got there. They made a big fuss over her hair, making her turn this way and that so they could see the purple lock from all angles.

"My mom would have a cow if I did that," Marybeth said enviously.

"My mom helped me do it," Sunshine told her.

"Don't talk about it," Carlie groaned.

Sunshine knew the other girls felt she was lucky to have a mother who let her do anything she wanted. Or almost anything, at least. She still wasn't sure about the nose piercing.

"Let's go order our Big Macs," she said. "I'm starved."

After they got their food, Sunshine pulled her sketches from the envelope and spread them over what space was left on the table. She wanted to get a decision made about the dresses before they started talking about Ducky Dumont.

"I've made three different designs," she said. "Look them over and see what you think. Mom and I have to start sewing them soon, or they'll never be finished in time for Pamela's wedding. My grandma said she'd help too."

She couldn't imagine that the other girls wouldn't like these designs. One was a dress whose skirt was short on one side but fell down to the floor on the other. On the short side, a triangle of material tacked to the shoulder hung down the back and sort of balanced the long side of the skirt. Another design was for a long, tight skirt with a top covered with ruffles. Sunshine thought of it as her "candle dress."

The third was her favorite. It featured a long, full skirt with an overblouse and a vest, a little bit like what Sunshine was wearing right now. Of course, the girls would be wearing slippers rather than combat boots, but otherwise the effect was the same.

Becca tapped a finger on the "candle dress." "I like this one," she said. "On our heads we could wear pointed hats, like flames."

She giggled, and so did the other Bee Theres.

Sunshine's face burned. They were making fun of her designs.

"These are just my first ideas," she said hurriedly. "I can make more."

"Hey," Becca said, "Ducky Dumont said if we needed a fashion consultant, just ask her."

She must have seen Sunshine's face then, because she said, "But we don't need her. You know, this one has possibilities." She touched the one with the diagonal skirt. "Maybe we could wear nylons that would match one of the colors of the dress."

Sunshine knew she was just trying to make her feel better.

Before anybody else could say anything, Becca said, "Speaking of Ducky Dumont . . . "

Sunshine expected her to finish with, "Let's talk about her." But instead, Becca said, " . . . here she is."

Sunshine looked up to see Ducky Dumont coming through the door with an attractive older woman who looked a lot like her.

Ducky spotted the Bee Theres right away. "Well, hey, dudettes," she sang out. "What's happening?"

"Hi, Ducky," the Bee Theres said in a chorus.

Ducky headed right over to their table. She still had her hair cornrowed with the beads on the ends, but today she wore ordinary blue jeans and a blue-and-white striped shirt. Even with plain clothes, she was still drop-dead gorgeous.

"This is my mom," she said, waving her hand toward the woman with her. "You guys look like you're holding a meeting or something."

Sunshine saw that the other Bee Theres felt as guilty as she did, because that was exactly what they *were* doing.

"We're having lunch," she said. "Want to join us? Both of you?" she added.

She had to say it. Sister Jackson would fry all of them if she ever found out they were rude to Ducky. Of course, Ducky would say no, since her mother wouldn't want to eat with a bunch of girls.

"Yes," Ducky said. She looked at the woman beside her. "Is that okay, Mom?"

Her mother nodded. "Sure, stay and eat with your friends."

"We were passing by when we saw the Golden Arches and just fell right in," Ducky said. "The last place we lived was so small, they didn't even have a McDonald's. Can you imagine?"

Without even pausing for breath, she said, "These are the girls in my Beehive class that I was telling you about, Mom. This is Marybeth. She's the executive type. Class president, you know. And Carlie, who's a real brain. Elena sings. I heard her during the closing song. Becca's great-great-grandma was a suffragette. Sunshine . . . "

Sunshine waited to see what Ducky would say about her.

She could feel the effect Ducky was having on the other girls. How could you dislike somebody who remembered so much about you after meeting you once?

Ducky didn't say anything for a moment. Sunshine looked up expectantly to see that she was staring at her.

"Girl, what have you done to your hair?" Ducky said finally. It wasn't hard after all to dislike Ducky.

But then Ducky said, "I love it. It's fabulous. And that dragon ear-cuff is terrific."

Sunshine felt as if she were on a roller coaster.

Suddenly she was ready to invite Ducky to join the Bee Theres.

But that was before Ducky spotted her dress designs.

CHAPTER
4

"Well, will you look at that!" Ducky said. She picked up the sketch of what Sunshine called her "candle dress." "You guys planning your Halloween costumes already?"

"Ducky!" her mother said.

Ducky looked up from the sketch, apparently noticing the absolute silence around the table. "Oh boy," she said. "I think I can taste my big, fat foot in my mouth."

Sunshine took the sketch from her. "I was just doodling. These are nothing." She gathered up the other sheets of paper.

"Yes, they are," Carlie said loyally. "Sunshine is designing our bridesmaids' dresses for Pamela's wedding. She's going to be a famous dress designer someday."

Sunshine wished Carlie hadn't gone quite that far. Now Ducky was going to really laugh.

But what Ducky did was groan. "I'm sorry. Mind if I go out of here and come in again so we can reshoot this scene?"

"You should, Ducky," her mother said. She looked around the table at each of the girls. "I'll run off and leave my rude daughter with you, if you can stand her. If she gets to be too much, ship her off home." With a smile, she left to go stand at the counter to order her lunch.

"I really am sorry," Ducky said. "I didn't mean to mouth off like that."

"It's okay. You don't need to apologize." Sunshine stuffed the drawings back into their envelope. They crumpled as she did so, but what did that matter?

Ducky shook her head. "No, it's not. Mom says my tongue is always out speeding down the freeway before my brain even gets out of the garage."

Becca and Elena giggled.

Well, let them laugh. Let them go off with Ducky. Sunshine bit her lower lip to keep it from trembling. She didn't care if they *all* went off with Ducky. Who needed the Bee Theres anyway?

She thought ahead to how it would be when she became a famous dress designer. She'd do it all by herself, and when Becca and Elena and the others came to one of her fashion shows in New York—no, make that Paris—they'd come running up to her and say, "Sunshine, remember when we were all in the Bee Theres Club together?" And she'd wrinkle her forehead and say, "I'm sorry. I can't recall anything like that. Have I ever met you before?"

She pushed back her chair, debating whether or not to stomp out of McDonald's. She'd eaten only half of her Big Mac and had scarcely started on the fries. It would be too embarrassing to gather them up to take with her. But she hated to leave them.

And she couldn't just sit there while the others made fun of her sketches.

Ducky put a hand on her arm. "Stay, girl. Don't you want to wait and see me squirm?" She smiled at Sunshine, showing all those perfect teeth of hers.

She was so good-natured about it that Sunshine pulled her chair close to the table again. Still feeling a little pouty, she twisted her lock of purple hair. "So squirm."

Ducky grinned again, then said, "I know what it's like to have people poke fun at what you want to do. Imagine how people used to laugh when I'd announce that someday I was going to be a famous model."

"Why would they laugh?" Becca asked. "You're beautiful. You *look* like a model."

Ducky rolled her eyes. "Maybe now. But you should have seen me a couple years ago. Skinny as a pencil. Toothpick legs. Teeth bigger than my face. Monster feet. Brillo hair. Believe me, I fit my name. Why do you think I call myself Ducky?"

She'd *chosen* the name? Sunshine had assumed her parents had given it to her and she couldn't do anything about it, the way her own parents had named her Sunshine.

"I'll bite," she said. "Why *do* you call yourself Ducky?"

Ducky leaned back in her chair. "Because I was the ugliest duckling in the pond. When I found I could make myself over into a swan, I decided to call myself Ducky so I'd always remember how it felt to have everybody laugh at my dreams." She looked at Sunshine. "And now I've been tromping all over yours. I'm really sorry for what I said."

For a long moment Sunshine returned her gaze. Then she said, "Well, Ducky, you're going to be back to being skinny as a pencil if you don't go get yourself some food."

Ducky laughed. "Had to get that foot out of my throat first." She stood up and headed for the counter. "Can I bring anybody anything?"

Nobody needed anything else. While Ducky was gone, Marybeth said, "I like her."

The others nodded.

"Should we invite her to be a Bee There?" Carlie asked.

"Let's wait a while," Becca said.

Maybe she was thinking about how Ducky might run for class office against her at school. But it wouldn't hurt to wait a while anyway. After all, Ducky didn't even know about the Bee Theres yet.

When Ducky got back with a cheeseburger, fries, and an orange drink, Sunshine took a deep breath and asked, "If you were designing bridesmaids' dresses, how would you do them?"

Ducky shrugged. "You know more about it than I do."

Sunshine swallowed, twisted her purple hair some more, and said, "I'd really appreciate some suggestions. *Really.*"

"What's the bride like?" Ducky asked.

Sunshine and the others spent several minutes telling how terrific Pamela was, how beautiful, how nice, how imaginative when it came to thinking of things their Beehive class could do.

Ducky chewed on a french fry. "What's *her* dress going to be like?"

Sunshine hadn't even thought of asking Pamela about that. It *would* be nice if the bridesmaids' dresses kind of fit in with what Pamela wore.

"I'll ask her," she said.

Ducky nodded. "I'd just make them something that will look great coming down the aisle ahead of the bride."

She bit off a big hunk of her cheeseburger, but she stopped chewing when everybody was silent again.

"Ooops," she said. "What did I do this time?"

Sunshine smiled as she shook her head. "Nothing. It's just that we won't be coming down the aisle. Pamela's going to be married in the Los Angeles Temple. We won't even be at the wedding."

Ducky looked puzzled as she swallowed what she was chewing. "How can you be bridesmaids if you're not at the wedding?"

"We'll be at the reception," Marybeth said.

"You mean," Ducky said, "that you won't walk down the aisle with the organ playing 'Here Comes the Bride' and carry bouquets and all that?"

"We'll have bouquets at the reception," Elena said.

That didn't seem to satisfy Ducky. "But why can't you be at the wedding?"

"You can't go to the temple until you're going to get married, or go on a mission, or at least are older than we are," Marybeth told her.

"You have to have a recommend," Carlie said.

Ducky still looked puzzled. "So isn't there somebody who can recommend you?"

Sunshine giggled along with the other Bee Theres. "I guess you don't quite understand," she said.

Ducky nodded. "I guess that's right. Those missionaries who taught me about the Church didn't get around to everything."

That worried Sunshine a little bit. She didn't want to say things all wrong and have Ducky quit the Church or something.

"Sister Jackson said we'll have a lesson on the temple soon," she said. "You'll learn about it then."

Maybe they'd *all* learn about it then. What Ducky had mentioned—walking down the aisle with all the flowers and music and everything—sounded so beautiful and so much fun that Sunshine wondered what could possibly make going to the temple a better way to get married.

"Well," Ducky said, "if you can't be at the wedding, then I'd make sure nobody will ever forget how you look at that reception."

After they finished eating, they all walked together down Lake Street. There weren't any stores to look at, unless Color Tiles turned you on. Mostly there were just fast-food places in that area. But nobody was ready to go home yet. School would be starting next week and they wouldn't be this free again for months.

They walked three across. Sunshine, Marybeth, and Elena were in front, with Carlie, Ducky, and Becca in back.

They were passing the fried-chicken place, and Ducky was telling Sunshine how good her purple hair looked in the sun, when suddenly they heard somebody singing. "There is SUNSHINE in my soul today, more glorious and bright . . . " It was a guy's voice, and it cracked when he sang "glorious."

Sunshine whirled around, trying to see who was singing. There were a couple of girls half a block behind them. Other than them, there was nobody else in sight except two big yellow chickens carrying signs that read "Eat at Buck-a-Cluck Chicken Shack."

One of the chickens came closer. "What happened to your hair? You fall in some grape juice or something?" It snickered as it stomped around on its big yellow feet.

Arvy Dixon! That's who it was. Arvy Dixon was inside that chicken suit! Sunshine could tell by his voice, and besides, that was the kind of thing Arvy would say.

"I don't talk to chickens," Sunshine said.

"That's discrimination," Arvy said from inside his

stupid chicken head, which had a high red comb and long red things that hung under his chin. "What do you have against us chickens?" He flapped his wings. "Bock-bock-bock-bock," he clucked.

"Let's go," Sunshine muttered.

"Why don't you hang out here for a while?" Arvy strutted around, clucking.

He stopped short in front of Ducky, and his chicken head bobbed as if he were trying to get a better view through the eye slots.

The other chicken, who'd been silently coming closer to the girls, collided with Arvy, and they both went down, tangled in their big chicken feet.

Ducky ran over to help them stand again.

Both of the chickens mumbled, "Thanks." Both of them stared at Ducky.

"Come on." Sunshine started to walk away, glancing back over her shoulder as they all left. The chickens were silent, still staring at Ducky.

Ducky laughed when the girls got a little distance away. "That first chicken likes you, Sunshine."

Sunshine stuck her tongue out and pointed down her throat to show what she thought of that.

Besides, it was clear to everybody, wasn't it, that both of the chickens were looking at Ducky?

So who cared who Arvy Dixon looked at?

Sunshine didn't care.

But within the last half hour Ducky had totally wiped out any ideas Sunshine had for the bridesmaids' dresses, and now she'd snatched away the only guy who'd ever paid any attention to Sunshine, even if it was only to sing, "There is sunshine in my soul today."

So what *were* they going to do about Ducky?

CHAPTER
5

Grandma was at the house when Sunshine got home. Sunshine could tell because Brunhilda was in the yard, barking her objections to being thrown out of the house. Grandma said dogs were animals and were supposed to be outside.

Sunshine stopped to soothe Brunhilda, then went into the house.

Grandma started right in. "Oh, my stars!" she exclaimed. "What have you done to your hair?" She reached out tentatively to touch the purple lock with one finger, as if it might slime her if she took hold of it. "Sunshine, your beautiful hair! Why would you do such a thing?"

"Let her alone, Mother," Sunshine's mom said. "I said it was okay."

Grandma threw up her hands as if to say that's

just what she'd expect from her daughter. "She looks like those strange creatures on TV," she said. She turned to Sunshine, this time touching her dragon ear-cuff, then stood back to look at her oversize purple shirt and droopy skirt. "You'll attract the wrong kind of people, doing things like this," she scolded.

Sunshine wondered if Grandma would think Ducky was the wrong kind of people, with her corn-rowed hair and strange clothes. Ducky had liked her purple hair and the ear-cuff.

"I'm glad to see you, Grandma," she said, stepping closer to kiss her on the cheek. "How long can you stay?"

"Don't change the subject, young lady," Grandma said. "You've got to get that gunk bleached out of your hair before Sunday. You can't go to church like that."

"Mother," Sunshine's mother said, "it's just something the kids do these days. It doesn't mean she's suddenly become an MTV freak or a Madonna groupie."

"Madonna groupie!" Grandma said scornfully. "In my day the Madonna was something sacred, and who-ever heard of groupies?"

Sunshine's mother put her hands on her hips. "You were a Frank Sinatra groupie, Mother. You've told me that a dozen times, how you used to scream and faint when you heard him sing."

"We *pretended* to faint," Grandma sniffed. "It was just something we did in those days."

Mom pointed a hand toward Sunshine. "And *this* is just something the kids do nowadays. They're just showing their individuality."

Sunshine wished they'd stop. Everything became a Big Deal when Grandma came to visit. There were always arguments as long as she was around. Grandma didn't like the way Sunshine and her mom lived. She didn't like the way they dressed or what they ate.

"Individuality!" she sniffed now. "In *my* day young girls were taught to be ladies, not to show their individuality."

Sunshine remembered seeing pictures in Grandma's albums of her as a young girl, dressed in grody suits with little hats and white gloves.

"Well," Sunshine's mother said, "I guess that means *something* has improved since those days."

That was like applying a match to a fuse.

Sunshine rushed to stop the explosion. "Grandma," she said, taking her arm. "Our class is having a really neat party next week about ancestors. We're supposed to dress like one of them, and bring food from one of their recipes. Do you have any suggestions about what I can do?"

Grandma sputtered a few times, like a firecracker fizzling out. Then she smiled and said, "Why, yes. I do have some suggestions."

Sunshine had figured she would. Grandma was really interested in genealogy and family history and that kind of stuff. She belonged to the Daughters of the Utah Pioneers, and she loved to talk about her ancestors.

"I have just the thing for you to wear," she said. "It's a patchwork dress that my grandmother—your great-great-grandmother—made for me back in 1947 when I was Centennial Queen in our little town in Idaho. Young people did *interesting* things back in those days. They didn't run around ruining themselves by dyeing their hair purple."

Sunshine let that go. "The dress sounds great, Grandma. Would you mind if I wear it?"

"If you'll be *very* careful," Grandma said. "It's an heirloom now."

Sunshine promised to be *very* careful.

Grandma pinched her lower lip, looking thoughtful. "There are shoes somewhere too. High-top, lace-up shoes. I wore them with the dress. Perhaps I can find them if I look."

Lace-up high-tops! Perfect!

"And recipes," Grandma went on. "Oh, yes, I've got lots of recipes. Have I ever made Quilter's Potato Salad for you?"

Sunshine shook her head.

"Well," Grandma said, "it was Grandmother's recipe. She used to make Quilter's Potato Salad whenever she had her friends come to her house to stitch up a quilt."

"I'm not big on potato salad," Sunshine said.

Grandma frowned. "Well, if you want to learn something about how your ancestors lived, maybe you should try eating what they ate. It wouldn't hurt you, you know. You'd ought to eat more food like that. It's a lot healthier than that french-fried garbage you young people eat." She paused. "And more nourishing than nuts and seeds and alfalfa sprouts." She looked pointedly at Sunshine's mom.

Sunshine's mom opened her mouth. They were about to start in again.

"Is it okay if I go to my room?" Sunshine said. "I have to draw some designs for our bridesmaids' dresses."

"I thought that's what you were doing last night," her mom said.

Grandma's eyes lit up. *Bridesmaids'* dresses! Oh, my goodness, I've got the *perfect* design for you. It's what my bridesmaids wore at my wedding reception back in 1948. I liked the design so much that I made an extra dress for myself, and I still have the pattern. The dress has a straight skirt with a peplum, sweetheart neckline, and puffed sleeves. The sweetest design you've ever seen."

Mentally, Sunshine stuck out her tongue and pointed down her throat. She didn't know what a peplum was, but the whole thing sounded awful.

But all she said was, "Thanks, Grandma. I'll come over in a couple of days and get the patchwork dress and shoes and the recipe."

Grandma looked happy now. "Fine. Come over on Sunday. Didn't I hear you say once that Pamela had sent the material for the dresses?"

Sunshine nodded.

"Bring it with you," Grandma instructed. "That way we can tell if the pattern would work well with that kind of material." She looked at Sunshine's head. "And while you're there, we'll bleach that purple stuff out of your beautiful hair."

No way.

Sunshine should have been happy about Grandma calling her hair beautiful, the way she'd wished her mom would when she'd first suggested dyeing part of it purple. But Grandma did it all wrong, being so bossy. It made Sunshine want to dig in her heels and resist.

As a small rebellion, she let Brunhilda come in the back door and go with her into her room.

Brunhilda wanted to play, probably to make up for the indignity of being locked out. She grabbed one of Sunshine's moose-shaped house slippers and danced around the room with it.

Sunshine loved those slippers, which her mom had given her on her last birthday, bought *new,* not at a garage sale. She tried to pull the slipper away from Brunhilda, but the dog just sank her teeth deeper into it, growling and shaking her head.

Sunshine finally had to substitute an old sneaker for the moose slipper before Brunhilda would give it up. After deciding that the slipper wasn't damaged except for a little dog spit, she put it and its mate inside her closet and shut the door.

Then she sat down to sketch a new design for the bridesmaids' dresses.

But Ducky had made her nervous. The dresses had to be flattering to all the Bee Theres. And they had to fit in with Pamela's dress.

The thing to do, then, was to write to Pamela and ask for a sketch of her wedding gown.

Sunshine dug into her school backpack until she found a pen. She didn't have any nice stationery, so she tore a page from a notebook.

"Dear Pamela," she wrote. "How are you? I am just fine."

She bit the end of the pen. How should she explain this whole thing? She wasn't good at putting words together, like Marybeth and Becca. Grandma would know what to write, but Sunshine wasn't about to ask her.

Why didn't she just *call* Pamela? What were telephones for, anyway?

She found the letter Pamela had sent, asking the Bee Theres to be bridesmaids. Her phone number in Idaho was there in the letter.

Sunshine went out into the hall where the telephone was. She was just going to pick it up when it rang.

"I'll get it," she yelled. "Hello?" she said into the phone.

"Uh . . . ," someone said. It sounded like a guy!

"Hello?" Sunshine repeated.

"Who's this?" the guy said.

"This is Sunshine."

"This is Arvy. Arvy Dixon."

Arvy! He was calling her! She'd never had a guy call her before.

Maybe Arvy *did* like her, the way Ducky said.

"Hi." Her voice sounded a little nervous. She cleared her throat and tried again. "Hi, Arvy."

"Hi."

There was a long pause.

"Arvy?" she said.

"Yeah?"

"I just wondered if you were still there, Arvy."

"Uh," he said. "Uh, Sunshine?"

"Yes?"

What was it he wanted to say to her? Did he want to say that he liked her?

Sunshine's heart beat faster.

Or was he going to sing that dumb song to her again?

"Uh," Arvy said again. "Like, uh, Sunshine, I was just wondering."

Wondering what? If she liked him, too? Was Arvy going to be her first boyfriend, even if she couldn't date him yet?

She heard him take a deep breath.

"I was wondering what that girl's name is," he said in a rush. "The one who was with you when you passed me and Jamahl in our chicken suits."

He was calling about Ducky! He wasn't interested in her, Sunshine, at all. He just wanted to know who Ducky was.

"Her name's Ducky," Sunshine said stiffly. "Ducky Dumont."

"Uh." Arvy still seemed to have trouble breathing.

"Uh, thanks. Jamahl wanted to know. I said I'd ask you."

Sure. *Jamahl* wanted to know. Right!

Out of the corner of her eye Sunshine saw Brunhilda sneak past her and head for the kitchen, where Mom and Grandma were.

"I gotta go, Arvy."

Drop dead, Arvy.

She was about hang up when he blurted, "That Ducky girl isn't as pretty as you are, Sunshine."

He hung up.

Sunshine stared at the phone in her hand. Had he really said what she thought he said?

A slow flush started somewhere down around her neck and spread up over her ears and cheeks.

Arvy Dixon *did* like her!

Grandma left soon after Sunshine saved her from gentle Brunhilda, who was lying placidly on the floor in the same room as Grandma.

"Remember now," Grandma said as she went out the door, "bring that material with you on Sunday."

"I will," Sunshine said, although her mind wasn't on the material. It was on Arvy Dixon.

It pleased her that Arvy wasn't totally dazzled by Ducky Dumont the way the other guys seemed to be. He liked *her*, Sunshine McGee.

On the other hand, what if he asked her for a date?

No, he wouldn't do that. He knew as well as she did that church policy said young people shouldn't date until they were sixteen.

But if he *did,* would Mom let her go? Mom knew

the policy too, but sometimes Mom made her own rules.

But probably that was one she wouldn't break.

Sunshine sighed. Life was SO complicated.

The thing she really had to concentrate on was the bridesmaids' dresses. She had to make another sketch, and she'd better hurry or Ducky might come up with one before she did.

She was worried about going to Grandma's house on Sunday to look at the bridesmaid's dress Grandma had saved from her own wedding. It was hard to say no to Grandma when she'd made up her mind, and she seemed so sure that the design of that dress would be right.

But Sunshine couldn't do anything about that until Sunday came.

Brunhilda followed her around with her leash in her mouth, asking to go for a walk.

She petted the dog and explained that first she had to call Pamela and find out what her wedding gown was like.

After asking Mom if it was okay, Sunshine dialed the phone number in Pocatello, Idaho, that Pamela had sent in her letter. Brunhilda flopped down on the floor and watched her, the leash still in her mouth.

The phone rang and rang, but nobody answered.

Sunshine was a little relieved. She needed to pull her wits together before she talked to Pamela. She'd call again on Sunday afternoon.

"Come on, Brunhilda," Sunshine said. "A walk is one thing I *can* do."

In their Beehive class on Sunday, Sister Jackson reminded the girls that the ancestor party was to be at her house on Wednesday night.

"We'll eat at five thirty," she said. "That way we can finish early so you can get your homework done, if you haven't done it already."

That sounded like a reminder to Get Your Homework Done Early. Sister Jackson didn't nag like Grandma, but she did occasionally throw in little digs like that.

Becca groaned. "Homework! School *starts* on Monday. We won't have homework that soon."

"Don't count on it," Ducky said. "My dad believes in having the teachers give homework the very first day."

Sunshine remembered that Ducky's dad was the new principal at the junior high they'd all be attending. Did that mean they'd be so loaded down with homework every night that there wouldn't be time for anything else? Right at the very time that she'd found out that Arvy Dixon LIKED HER?

And what about the bridesmaids' dresses? When would she have time to design them, to say nothing of getting them sewn?

"Can't you talk your dad out of it?" she asked Ducky. "We need to kind of ease back into homework after being off all summer."

Ducky snorted. "Talk him out of it? Girl, you don't know my dad. He thinks school is for *learning!*"

Now everybody groaned, except for Sister Jackson.

Sunshine couldn't help thinking that life would have been simpler if Ducky and her family had never shown up.

On the other hand, it was kind of interesting to have a girl like Ducky in the class. Today she had taken her hair out of the cornrows and pulled it to the top of her head. She'd wrapped a bright scarf around it so that it looked a little like a fountain, spraying up a little way and then falling back in a smooth flow around her head. No matter what Ducky did, she looked spectacular.

Sunshine wondered how *she* would look with a hairdo like that. Maybe she could color a few more strands of her hair and just have the purple part standing up.

With her luck, it would just look like a giant purple mushroom sprouting out of her head.

Sister Jackson was looking at her, which meant she knew Sunshine's attention was wandering. Sister Jackson never missed anything.

"When *I* taught school," Sister Jackson was saying, "I assigned homework the first day. I agree with your father, Ducky. School is for learning, and you might as well get right to it."

This was the first time Sister Jackson had mentioned that she'd taught school. Probably she'd done just about everything, since she'd lived so many years.

"What did you teach?" Sunshine asked, mainly to show that her attention hadn't wandered off too far.

"Home economics," Sister Jackson said. "Food preparation, sewing, home decoration, child care— things like that."

It figured. That's why she was so good at cooking and all those other things.

Had she ever designed dresses? Maybe she could help Sunshine design a dress that everybody would like better than what Ducky might suggest.

How could Sunshine ask her for help without really letting on that she *needed* help?

Sunshine didn't hear much of the lesson. Her mind shuffled instead from worrying about the bridesmaids' dresses to wondering whether Arvy Dixon would be waiting for her downstairs. She hadn't seen him with the other Scouts before class.

"What do you think, Sunshine?" Sister Jackson asked.

Sunshine didn't know what she was supposed to think *about*. Were they still talking about homework?

"Well," she said, "I guess I'd have to say . . . " What *could* she say? "I mean, when it comes right down to it, I think maybe, if I had to make a choice, uh . . ."

Sister Jackson waited patiently. All the other Beehives were looking at Sunshine.

She cleared her throat. "I guess what I really want to say is, you know, that the way things are, I think I would probably gain a lot by doing it."

Sister Jackson's expression didn't change, but Sunshine heard a little gasp from one of the girls.

"Thank you, Sunshine," Sister Jackson said. "Would anybody else like to comment?"

Marybeth's hand shot up. "I'd *never* read my sister's diary," she said firmly. "In the first place, she'd kill me, and in the second place, I'd die if she read mine, and in the third place a diary is *private*."

Diaries! They'd been talking about *diaries!* About reading your sister's diary, she guessed. In fact, Sister Jackson held a newspaper clipping in her hand. Probably the same Dear Abby column that Sunshine had read with the letter from the girl who objected that her sister read her diary.

Sunshine's face burned a little as she thought of

what she'd just said. She'd said she'd probably gain a lot by doing it.

Her thoughts were in a jumble. She wished she'd just admitted she hadn't been listening. She wished Arvy Dixon would ride into the room on a white horse and carry her away from there.

"Let's go on," Sister Jackson said. "So if you wouldn't read your sister's diary, Marybeth, is it all right to read your great-grandmother's diary?"

Carlie raised her hand. "Sure, as long as she's dead and left it behind."

Becca giggled. "What if she died and took it with her?"

Sister Jackson spoke over the laughter. "The point is, while a person is alive, a diary is a private thing. Sometimes we put our most private thoughts into a diary, and we don't want anybody else to read it. If we find something in an ancestor's diary that would embarrass her, perhaps we shouldn't make it public. But if you have an old diary, pick a passage that reveals something about the writer and copy it off for our ancestor party on Wednesday night."

Becca nodded. "I've got my great-great-grand-mother's journal. She was one of the first women doctors in Utah."

Ducky grinned. "One of my ancestors was a conjure woman, and my dad has her little book of magic spells."

"Wow," breathed Elena. "I'd like to hear some of them."

Sunshine felt a little irked. Everything about Ducky was different from everybody else. What was *she* going to do to win back her reputation of being the different one?

Maybe she could be the first one to go on a date with a guy.

Very likely Ducky had already done that, since until she joined the Church, she didn't know about the no-dating-until-you're-sixteen rule.

Sister Jackson closed her lesson book.

"Now, we need to discuss a few things about Sister Spencer's wedding," she said. "She called me last week, since I'm going to coordinate things here." She looked at Ducky. "Forgive us, Ducky, if we just have a few words about this. By the way, I told her about you, and she's anxious to meet you."

Ducky looked pleased. "I'm anxious to meet her too. She sounds really nice. And please go ahead and talk about the wedding. Maybe I can help in some way. I was a bridesmaid when my aunt got married last summer."

Well, of course Ducky had been a bridesmaid. She'd probably designed all the dresses and fixed all the food too.

"I'm sure there will be some way you can help,"

Sister Jackson said. She looked at Sunshine. "Pamela asked about the dresses. Do you need any help with them, Sunshine?"

"No," Sunshine said quickly.

Why had she said that? Of course she needed help. Why hadn't she admitted that she was feeling desperate and needed all the help she could get?

"That's fine," Sister Jackson said. "Marybeth, will you please assign somebody to give the closing prayer?"

On the way downstairs Marybeth asked Sunshine if she would really read her sister's diary—if she had a sister, and if the sister kept a diary, and if she happened to find it.

"I don't have a sister," Sunshine said, "so how would I know?"

She thought the girls looked at her suspiciously, all except for Ducky. Ducky walked by her side and whispered, "You were a million miles away today, girl. Is there something wrong?"

How did Ducky know she'd been a million miles away? Was she a conjure woman like her ancestor?

Sunshine wanted to say, "Oh yes, please, Ducky, please help me design the bridesmaids' dresses." But that would just be giving Ducky one more triumph.

"No," Sunshine said. "I don't need help with anything. Thanks anyway, Ducky."

Arvy Dixon wasn't waiting for her downstairs. Was he sick or something? Was he too embarrassed even to talk to her after his admission yesterday that he liked her?

Sunshine hoped the rest of the day would be better than the first part.

She called Pamela in Idaho when she got home. This time Pamela answered. She sounded breathless. It reminded Sunshine a whole lot of how she used to come running in to class, puffing and panting, always just a minute or two late. It seemed as if Pamela crammed her life with exciting events, and there were always a few too many to squeeze into twenty-four hours. She was so different from Sister Jackson.

"Sunshine!" Pamela said when Sunshine identified herself. "How wonderful to hear from you!"

"We miss you," Sunshine said.

"I miss you too. I'll be seeing you very soon, though."

"I know." Sunshine felt a little panicky. She decided not to tell Pamela that she didn't even have a clue about the bridesmaids' dresses yet. "I was just wondering about your wedding dress. We want to kind of make our dresses to match somehow."

"How smart of you, Sunshine, to think of that!

Oh, it's the most beautiful dress ever." Pamela sounded happy. "My mother and Grandma Louisa have been helping me with it."

"What does it look like?" Sunshine asked.

"Well, mainly it's Grandma Louisa's wedding dress. She got married in the forties, but she was into old-fashioned, so it looks as if it came from pioneer days or something." Pamela's voice was dreamy. "It's got a skirt that's fitted in front but then draped in back so it's very graceful. It has kind of a little bustle and a train with a thingy that I hook onto my middle finger when I don't want it dragging behind me." She laughed. "Sunshine, you're the one who knows about fashions. I'm sure you know all the right words for what I'm describing."

It seemed to Sunshine that everybody had a lot more confidence in her than she had in herself. But she wasn't going to admit that she didn't know as much as they thought she did. She didn't know as much as *she* had thought she did!

"What's the bodice like?" she asked. That was one word she knew.

"It's fitted, with buttons down the back," Pamela said. "There's a sort of high collar and then, you know, those tight sleeves that come to a point over the hands."

Sunshine tried to picture the dress. "Sounds wonderful."

"It is. We're decorating it with some lace that's about the only thing left from my Great-grandmother Tabitha's wedding dress."

"Tabitha?" Sunshine hadn't heard that name before.

"Don't you love it?" Pamela said. "And I'm wearing my mother's veil. Kind of a patchwork wedding outfit, wouldn't you say? So as far as the bridesmaids' dresses are concerned, just make them so they'll fit in with what I've described. I'm sending you whatever lace is left over from Great-grandmother Tabitha's dress. If you can find a place to put some on whatever you've got going, I'd love it."

Sunshine didn't mention that she didn't have anything going. "That's what I needed to know," she said.

They talked for a little longer, then hung up.

Sunshine thought about the name Tabitha. Did that fit her? Maybe she could recycle Pamela's great-grandmother's name as well as the lace on her dress.

She felt better about the dresses as she got ready to go to her grandmother's house. Now that she knew what Pamela's wedding gown was like, she could tell for sure if the style of the dress Grandma had been talking about would fit in with it.

Maybe it would. Maybe it would be just perfect,

since Grandma had been married in the forties too, like Pamela's grandmother.

Wouldn't it be nice if the dress pattern *was* perfect? It would make Grandma happy, and Sunshine wouldn't have to figure out how to stop her from taking over. She'd also have a design ready before Ducky would, and she wouldn't have to admit to Sister Jackson that she needed help.

The first thing Grandma did when Sunshine arrived at her house with the dress material was drag her off to her bedroom.

"I found both my patchwork dress and the bridesmaid's dress from my wedding. You'll absolutely love them," she assured Sunshine.

The dresses were hanging on the back of the bedroom door, draped with a sheet.

Sunshine held her breath as Grandma pulled off the sheet. She kept holding it as she stared at the bridesmaid's dress.

"What did I tell you?" Grandma said. "You're speechless. Your problems are over. We can start sewing tomorrow."

Sunshine was speechless all right. But she didn't think her problems were over.

CHAPTER 7

In the first place, the bridesmaid's dress was maroon. Dark maroon. In the second place, it was made of stiff taffeta. And in the third place, it was fussy. It had maroon lace around the sweetheart neckline and on the edges of the elbow-length sleeves. The skirt was ankle length and straight with kind of a short overskirt, which was also edged with maroon lace.

"My wedding reception was so beautiful." Grandma's eyes were a little misty. "I had six bridesmaids. Each one wore a dress like this, and my dress was just like it only all white."

Sunshine didn't know what to say. The thought of six dresses like this one, all in one room together, boggled her mind.

"I've got my wedding picture around here someplace," Grandma said, going to a piece of furniture she called a secretary. Opening a drawer, she stirred around in it for a moment, then pulled out a photograph in a cardboard frame.

She came back to Sunshine, holding it up. "We were married just three years after World War II ended, and Mac wore his Navy lieutenant's uniform for the reception."

Sunshine had seen the photograph before, but she hadn't really looked at it closely. It was black and white, so you couldn't see the color of the dresses. In the picture they just looked dark and totally hideous.

But the bridesmaids were all slender, with cute faces framed by sausage curls or what Grandma called pompadour hairdos. The bridegroom and the best man both wore white uniforms, which looked very romantic.

It was hard to imagine Grandma ever being as young as the lovely bride with the blonde hair that curled under at the ends. A pageboy, Grandma called the hairstyle. But even though she was old now, her eyes and nice teeth, which she displayed in a wide smile in the photograph, were still the same.

"You were so pretty, Grandma," Sunshine said. "May I take this to show at our ancestors party too?"

Grandma looked pleased. "Well, sure you can, if you want to." She laughed. "I have a problem thinking of myself as an ancestor, but I guess that's what I am." She looked at the old photograph, then at Sunshine. "You know what, Sunshine? I see a resemblance. Your mouth is like mine, and your teeth. You look a lot like I did then."

Now it was Sunshine's turn to be pleased. Was she really as pretty as Grandma had been all those years ago?

She hugged Grandma. "I'd love to look like you," she said.

Sometimes Grandma was so terrific. With all these compliments flying around, maybe she would forget that she was trying to push Sunshine into using her bridesmaid's dress pattern.

But Grandma didn't forget.

"You girls will look just as pretty as we did," she said, "when we get you all dolled up in dresses like this." She waved a hand at the maroon bridesmaid's dress. "And when we get that hideous purple out of your hair."

Sunshine put a hand up to her hair, but Grandma went on. "If we really apply ourselves, we can cut a pattern from this bridesmaid's dress. Then we can get to work on your dresses."

Sunshine wondered if she was going to go into her "apply yourself" lecture, a familiar one with

Grandma. Sunshine didn't want to hear any more of it.

"Uh," she began, "Grandma . . . " She touched the short overskirt on the dress. "What do you call this?" She was stalling for time until she could think of how to tell Grandma they for sure didn't want to use her pattern.

"A peplum," Grandma said. "I've noticed they've been coming back into fashion, so you'll be right up-to-date."

"You know what, Grandma?" Sunshine said. "Actually, Pamela's dress is quite old-fashioned look-ing, and we may decide we don't want anything as up-to-date as a dress with a peplum."

Grandma fluttered a hand. "Peplums reappear every few years. This style of dress could be adapted to fit almost any year."

Sunshine felt a little frantic. "I'll have to talk with the other Beehives about it. I have to let them help me make the decision."

Grandma opened her mouth, but before she could say anything, Sunshine changed the subject. "Let's look at the patchwork dress your grandmother made for you now, shall we? The one I want to wear on Wednesday night?"

"You *could* wear the bridesmaid's dress," Grandma said, "and show the others how it looks."

"I already told everybody I'd be wearing the patchwork dress," Sunshine hurried to say. "And I'd like to see your mother's journal, if you found it."

"All right," Grandma said reluctantly.

When she got home, Sunshine could hardly wait to show the patchwork dress to her mom.

"Did you know Grandma had this neat dress hanging way back in her closet?" she asked.

Mom smiled. "I wore it once when I was in a state speech contest. I called my speech 'Patchwork,' and I used the dress to illustrate what I was saying. I won first place."

Someday Sunshine would ask Mom to tell her about the speech, but not now. She took the dress from the zippered bag Grandma kept it in. "Grandma said her grandmother made it from scraps of material from her ragbag," she said. "Each piece has a story. She wore the dress when she was Centennial Queen in her ward back in 1947. That's when the whole church celebrated the one hundredth anniversary of Brigham Young and the Saints arriving in Salt Lake Valley."

She realized she was sounding like a Sunday School teacher, but Grandma's story about the dress had been interesting. "It fits perfectly," she said, "even though Grandma was older than I am when she wore it."

"Girls are bigger nowadays," Mom said. "By the way, what did you do about Grandma's bridesmaid's dress?"

Sunshine sighed. "It won't do."

Mom nodded. "I know. But how did you convince *her?*"

"I didn't," Sunshine admitted. "I have to figure out a way to do it without hurting her feelings. She can be *so* stubborn sometimes."

Mom nodded again. "Just like somebody else I know," she said with a smile.

School started on Monday. Mr. Dumont, Ducky's father who was the new principal at the junior high, spoke at an assembly for all students. He was very pleasant, but he talked about how he believed school was for learning and that he was instructing teachers to assign lots of homework.

All of the Bee Theres and Ducky were sitting together in the front of the auditorium.

"What did I tell you?" Ducky said.

Everybody was groaning all over the auditorium.

Mr. Dumont held up a hand to quiet them. "Someday you'll thank me," he said, "when you get out of school and you've got the jump on a lot of people because you've applied yourselves."

He smiled as he said it, but you could tell he wasn't going to change his mind.

"He sounds like Grandma," Sunshine said.

Ducky slid down in her seat. "Tell me about it," she moaned. "It's going to be a tough year."

Thinking about Grandma reminded Sunshine of the bridemaid's dress, which took her thoughts to the fact that she had to decide immediately on *some* kind of a pattern for the bridesmaids' dresses for Pamela's wedding, or they would never get finished in time.

Anything would be better than Grandma's pattern.

She didn't have much time the rest of the day to think about it, what with all her new classes. She liked her math teacher, but she could tell her English class was going to be a pain. In her gym class they played soccer, which was Sunshine's favorite sport because she was good at it. But Ducky was in the same class, and somebody who'd known her before she moved there announced that she'd been known as The Tornado on her middle-school soccer team.

Was Ducky the best at *everything?*

On Wednesday a small parcel arrived in the mail from Pamela. In it was a long piece of fragile, cream-colored lace, a picture, and a letter.

"The lace," Pamela wrote, "is what I told you about on the phone, from my great-grandmother's wedding dress. We put some on my maid-of-honor's dress too, so we'll all match just a little. Sort of symbolic or something. Don't ask me what it's symbolic of, because my brain is short-circuited these days."

She'd drawn a happy-face after that sentence, so it didn't seem to matter that she was short-circuited.

The picture was of her wedding dress hanging on the back of a door. It looked as if it was all finished.

That panicked Sunshine again. How was she going to get time to think up a dress design, to say nothing of getting them all sewn, with all that homework Mr. Dumont had prescribed coming toward her?

She was still worrying about it as she dressed for the ancestors party that night. But she pushed it to the back of her mind when she saw herself in the mirror.

The pastel colors of the patchwork dress suited her perfectly, as if they'd been planned for her. The dress was made in two pieces, with a top that buttoned down the front and came to a point in the back. It was lined and had a small white collar.

The skirt was sort of straight in front but had a lot of fullness in back where it fell gracefully to the floor. Walking back and forth in front of the mirror, Sunshine felt tall and elegant, even though the dress was made of scraps.

Along with the dress, Grandma had given her the high-top black shoes that had belonged to some ancestor a long time ago. They pinched a little, but Sunshine was able to wear them. Along with the shoes, she had a reticule, a little purse with a long strap, almost like the small shoulder purses she and her friends carried. The reticule was made from patchwork that matched the dress.

Mom helped with her hair, French-braiding it so that it was pulled back away from her face. The purple streak was blended in with the rest of her hair, giving it an interesting effect.

Sunshine was sure she'd be the prettiest "ancestor" at the party.

She also had her great-grandmother's diary from which she'd selected a passage to read to the other girls. She took along the stuff from Pamela too, and Grandma's wedding picture, and, of course, the Quilter's Potato Salad Grandma had helped her make.

The first thing Sunshine saw when Mom dropped her off at Sister Jackson's house was that Sister Jackson had once again asked some of the Scouts to come help her serve the dinner. She'd done that for the very first dinner she'd had for the Beehive class, right after she became their teacher. It had been a disaster because the girls had been trying to get rid of Sister

Jackson then, and they'd all dressed in grungy and weird outfits to show her that she couldn't possibly handle a bunch like them. The boys had been dressed in their Sunday clothes, and they'd been on their best behavior, so the whole thing had been very embarrassing.

But this was different. The girls were all dressed like their ancestors. Even the Scouts seemed to be dressed like ancestors, with dark pants, white shirts, suspenders, and little round-topped black hats.

Arvy Dixon was there. Sunshine hadn't seen him since the phone call when he'd said she was prettier than Ducky.

She was sure he'd think she was pretty tonight.

The next thing she noticed was that Ducky was the center of attention again. She was dressed in something really ethnic. It was a long, bright-colored, striped robe. With it she wore a close-fitting round hat and a necklace made from big brown pods. She was barefoot but wore some kind of decoration around one ankle.

She made Sunshine suddenly feel pale and colorless, the way she'd felt on the first day Ducky came to their Beehive class.

The third thing Sunshine noticed was that Ducky's eyes lit up as she watched her walk in.

"Sunshine," Ducky said, "I know exactly what your design for the bridesmaids' dresses should be."

Sunshine had just *known* that if she didn't figure out a design really fast, Ducky would beat her to it. It was humiliating after she'd bragged that she didn't need any help. She felt her face reddening as she said, "You're a little late, Ducky. I already have a design."

She was going to have to use Grandma's pattern. It was either that or let Ducky take over.

Ducky looked disappointed when Sunshine said she already had a design for the bridesmaids' dresses. In fact, she looked so disappointed that Sunshine figured she really must have wanted to do it herself.

"Well," Ducky said, "I hope it's as good as what you've got on."

What did she mean? Ducky was looking at the patchwork dress Sunshine wore, examining the back, reaching out to adjust the collar just a little. Carlie, Marybeth, Becca, and Elena were looking at it from all angles too.

"This is one neat design," Ducky said. "And it just might work for Pamela's wedding."

Ducky was talking about the design of the patchwork dress! Why hadn't Sunshine thought of that? She looked down at herself. She'd been so uptight about Grandma's ugly maroon thing that she hadn't even thought about copying this pattern.

"Well, what design did you think I was going to use?" Juggling the bowl with the potato salad, the plastic bag with the lace, and the other things she'd brought, Sunshine did a little twirl in front of all the girls. She wasn't exactly telling a lie, was she? She just wasn't saying that the idea of using this pattern had occurred to her only after Ducky put it into her head.

Becca and Carlie looked at the back of the dress and squealed. "It makes your waist look about eighteen inches around," Becca said. "We're going to look so *neat* in dresses made from this pattern."

"All in that pretty material Pamela sent," Carlie added.

Sunshine held up the plastic bag she'd brought with her. "With some of this lace on each one. It's from the dress Pamela's great-grandmother wore at her wedding."

She was aware that the Scouts were watching from the doorway to the kitchen.

Dale Delancy started prancing around. "Do you like these black suspenders?" he asked in a high voice. "Or do you think I should have worn my pink-and-blue striped ones?"

Gregory Okinaga picked up on it. "How about my hat? It used to belong to my great-grandfather's uncle's dentist's brother's horse. He wore it when he pulled the ice wagon." He strutted around the room, wagging his head so that the round-topped hat almost fell off.

Arvy Dixon didn't say anything. He didn't look at Sunshine either.

She was glad. Remembering what he'd said about thinking she was pretty, she would have blushed if he'd looked at her. It had sounded nice over the telephone, but now that she was in the same room with Arvy, she was embarrassed.

"Boys," Sister Jackson said, coming from the kitchen, "come help me, please. Arvy, will you take the bowl from Sunshine and bring it with you?"

Still not looking at her, Arvy came over and reached out for the bowl. Sunshine looked away as she handed it to him. She thought he had hold of it, but when she let go, it dropped to the floor.

There was a gasp from the other girls as the bowl with the potato salad landed upside down. Sunshine and Arvy both grabbed for it at the same time, knocking heads painfully together as they bent over.

"No harm done," Becca said, as she lifted the bowl from the floor right side up. "The lid stayed on."

No harm done! Didn't she hear the loud klonk from their heads hitting together? Sunshine's head hurt, and so did her dignity. She was embarrassed too, not so much about touching heads with Arvy but about the loud noise. It sounded as if their heads were hollow or something.

And Sister Jackson was there, rubbing first her head, then his, as if they were little kids. "You're going to have a couple of matching goose eggs," she said, "but you'll be all right."

Sunshine wished she hadn't said that. The other guys were sure to remember it and yell it all over school tomorrow that she and Arvy Dixon had twin goose eggs.

Maybe she'd stay home from school.

She sneaked a look at Arvy, whose face was on fire. He was rubbing his head. "Oh, I'm sorry," he mumbled.

"It's okay," she mumbled back.

She couldn't believe that just a couple days ago she'd been so excited to think he liked her. She'd even wondered if her mom would let her go out on a date with him before she was sixteen. And worst of all, she'd written "Mrs. Arvy Dixon" all over a notebook page one night when she was alone in her room. She'd torn it up immediately, of course, but it made her blush to think she'd ever done a thing like that.

"If you're all right now," Sister Jackson said, "let's have dinner."

Arvy and the other guys disappeared into the kitchen, and Sunshine had time to pull her wits back together. Things weren't *all* bad. She finally had the right design in mind for the bridesmaids' dresses.

This dinner wasn't as formal as the first one Sister Jackson had invited the Beehives to. That one had been to prepare them for the Couth Youth banquet, but this one was just for fun.

Sister Jackson had put various "ancestor" things in the middle of her big dining-room table. There was an old-fashioned photograph of a young couple, solemn and stiff-looking, posing for what Sister Jackson said was their wedding picture back in 1885. Sunshine put Grandma's wedding picture beside it, and the other girls exclaimed over how pretty she'd been.

There was a small wooden chest with letters addressed in fading ink spilling out of it. A pressed rose lay across an old diary, and there was a porcelain figure of a girl feeding a goose.

The table was set with flowered dishes that Sister Jackson said had belonged to her grandmother. The pretty linen napkins had been embroidered by another relative many years ago.

After the girls were seated, Sunshine had time to look around at what the others had worn. The only one she'd had time to notice so far was Ducky.

Becca wore a high-necked black dress that she said had been her great-great-grandmother's, the one who'd been a suffragette a hundred years ago. Carlie wore her grandmother's Japanese kimono, and her hair was arranged on top of her head with a couple of long things that looked almost like knitting needles stuck into it.

Marybeth looked cute in the dress her great-great-great-grandmother had brought across the plains in a handcart. And Elena wore an embroidered Mexican blouse and tiered red skirt that she said had belonged to her grandmother's sister who had been a folk dancer.

It was fun to sit there wearing things that had so many stories attached to them. It was as if the people who'd owned them were somehow continuing on in life.

Well, of course, *some* of them were still alive, like Carlie's grandmother. And Sunshine's own grandmother, who owned the patchwork dress.

Thinking of Grandma made Sunshine sigh with relief that now she wouldn't have to come right out and tell her she didn't like the pattern of the maroon bridesmaid's dress. She'd just say that she liked this design better, and since it also belonged to Grandma, Sunshine was sure she would be pleased about it.

The dinner—with English "bubble and squeak,"

German spaetzle, Mexican tamales, African peanut salad, Japanese marinated cucumbers, and Sunshine's Quilter's Potato Salad—was delicious.

The Scouts brought in all the food, then sat down at the places Sister Jackson had provided for them at the long table. They started a conversation comparing scabs they'd acquired from various small accidents, but Sister Jackson said that wasn't suitable at the table. She said they should remember something about *their* ancestors.

Dale Delancy said his great-great-grandfather had been a frontier doctor who had learned medicine by cutting up bodies of criminals after they'd been hung.

Sister Jackson changed the subject again, and they talked about movies and TV programs until the dinner was over.

Arvy Dixon mostly looked at his plate as he ate, although once Sunshine saw him sneak a glance at her. She wished he wouldn't look at her. She wasn't ready to have a boyfriend yet, she decided.

After dinner, Sister Jackson had the boys take the dishes out to the kitchen and wash them while she and the girls sat in the living room and had their program.

"Each of us," Sister Jackson said, "is like Sunshine's dress, made up of patchwork from all of our ancestors. We are products of the past. By studying our ancestors, we can come to know ourselves better."

She looked around the circle of girls. "Someday you will all be ancestors, and perhaps your granddaughters will be passing along something that came from you, and that's why it's important for you to keep journals and pass along your experiences and what you've learned from life."

Sunshine smiled to herself. She was going to write this whole thing about the bridesmaids' dresses in her journal. She wasn't sure yet what she'd learned from it, but it was a good story.

"So," Sister Jackson said, "now we'll each take our turn presenting excerpts from an ancestor's diary or a story from them or whatever you brought."

Marybeth read from an old journal that was made from brown wrapping paper, cut into pages and sewn together down the middle. She said her great-great-great-grandmother hadn't had any regular paper out on the plains of Nebraska, so she'd taken this way to record her experiences. She'd told about being at Winter Quarters after the Saints had been driven out of Nauvoo.

Elena sang an old folk song in Spanish that she said had been passed down through her family for many years.

Becca read one of the speeches her great-great-grandmother had made about passing an amendment to the Constitution to give women the vote.

Carlie put a tape of Japanese music on Sister Jackson's tape deck and did a traditional dance that she said was part of her family heritage.

Sunshine read the part she'd marked in her great-grandmother's diary where she told about how much she liked the boy who sat behind her in school. "Harvey yanks my hair," she'd written, "so I know he loves me."

Everybody laughed.

Then Sunshine read from a later passage. "Harvey and I are the only ones left in the mathematics contest," her great-grandmother had written. "Will he still like me if I beat him? Maybe I should lose, just in case he won't like it if a girl does better than he does."

The girls leaned forward with interest. "What did she do?" Ducky asked.

Sunshine flipped a few more pages. "I won the contest," she read from the diary. "Harvey didn't say anything to me."

"Male chauvinist pig," Becca muttered, grinning.

Sunshine smiled. "Seven years later he married her," she said. "So I guess he liked smart girls."

"Nice story," Ducky said.

But once again Ducky was the star of the show with an African folktale about "The Girl with Large Eyes" who married a fish. It had been handed down through the family from the ancestor who traveled the Underground Railway to escape slavery.

Sunshine didn't mind that everybody liked Ducky's contribution the best. She was very grateful to Ducky for making her realize that the patchwork dress design would be perfect for the bridesmaids' dresses.

"Now," Sister Jackson said when the program was over, "now we all have little patches of other cultures in the fabric of our lives."

Sunshine went home feeling happy.

She didn't call Grandma that night to tell her about her decision to use the design of the patchwork dress. She still had some homework to do, thanks to Ducky's dad's rule at school. She was tired when she finished and went to bed.

Just as she'd figured, the next day Dale Delancy blatted all over school that she and Arvy Dixon had twin goose eggs on their heads. It was so embarrassing. She didn't see Arvy, except for a glimpse of him in the cafetorium at lunch. She didn't *want* to see him.

She was glad when school was over and she could gather up Grandma's stuff and go to her house.

Grandma met her at the door with a big smile. "I'm glad you've come," she said. "We can start on your dresses this very day."

Sunshine nodded. "I know. Grandma, I've decided . . . "

Grandma interrupted. "I've already cut out three dresses, for you and Carlie and Marybeth, since I know all your sizes. If you'll have the other girls come over, I'll cut theirs out too. You can sit right down and start to sew."

As she spoke, she led Sunshine into her bedroom, where the cut-out pieces of three dresses lay on the bed. There they were, sweetheart necklines, skinny skirts, and peplums, all ready to sew.

CHAPTER
9

Sunshine couldn't say a thing. If she'd so much as opened her mouth, she would have started bawling. To hide what she was feeling, she went to Grandma's closet and hung the pretty patchwork dress inside. If only she'd recognized on Sunday that *this* was the design she should use for the bridesmaids' dresses!

Grandma bustled about happily.

"I thought we'd sew your dress up today," she said. "It won't take long to whip it together. Then when the other girls come to be measured, you can model it for them."

Sunshine imagined modeling the peplum dress for the other Beehives. She imagined what they'd say, especially Becca, who had a runaway mouth.

"So," Grandma said, "why don't you start pinning the pieces together and I'll start sewing." She picked up one set of pieces and handed them to Sunshine. "Start with the skirt," she said, "while I go fix us a little snack."

She hurried off toward the kitchen.

Sunshine stood there holding the pieces of the dress. A couple of tears ran down her cheeks. She couldn't help it. This was a total, out-and-out, megadisaster, and her numb brain couldn't think of a thing she could do about it.

Except sew the dress. Do as Grandma said. Don't think.

Maybe she'd be pleasantly surprised when she tried it on. Maybe it was the maroon color that made Grandma's bridesmaid's dress look so bad. Maybe the lovely peachy colors of Pamela's material would look good even with the peplum design.

Sunshine opened Grandma's little handkerchief drawer and took one of her neatly ironed, cedar-smelling hankies. Grandma kept cedar eggs in the drawer; and ever since she'd been little, Sunshine had thought it was so much more interesting to use one of her hankies when you needed one than to pull out a plain old tissue.

Wiping her eyes and blowing her nose, she deposited the hankie in the laundry hamper, then picked up the box of pins Grandma had set out and went to work fitting the pieces of the dress together.

Grandma came back soon with a plate of peanut butter and brown sugar sandwiches, cut up into tiny, bite-size squares. When she was little, Sunshine had loved to come to Grandma's and have tea parties with the tiny sandwiches and cocoa, which the two of them drank out of itty-bitty cups that Grandma had had when she was a child.

Things had been so much simpler then.

Sunshine bit her lips so she wouldn't start blubbering again. "Here's the skirt all pinned together," she said, handing the pieces to Grandma.

It didn't take Grandma long to "whip the dress together." Sunshine had always admired the way she sewed, feeding the cloth into the chopping needle at high speed, rounding curves without slowing down, racing to the finish, then biting off the threads before she held the completed product up for Sunshine to admire.

Sunshine tried to admire the dress as it took shape. She choked on one of the little peanut butter sandwiches when she tried to say, in answer to Grandma's comment, that yes, the dress did look different as it went together. What she wanted to say was that she liked it better in pieces.

Her opinion didn't change when Grandma bit off the last thread and held up the dress, finished except for putting in the long back zipper and the hem.

"There, isn't that beautiful?" Grandma said. "Try it on, Sunshine."

There wasn't anything for her to do but shuck off her blue jeans and T-shirt and pull on the dress.

Grandma positioned her in front of the long mirror on her closet door, pulling the back together and pinning it shut.

Sunshine looked at herself. The sweetheart neckline made her long neck look as scrawny as a chicken's, and the bodice emphasized the fact that she had no chest to speak of. The peplum stuck out like a shelf around her hips. The straight skirt fell almost down to her thick ankle socks and scuffed white Nikes.

Even Grandma was silent as she gazed at Sunshine's reflection in the mirror.

"It will look better when we get the zipper in." She pulled the back a little closer together. "And you could stuff a few tissues in your bra."

"I don't have a bra," Sunshine confessed miserably.

"We'll get you one," Grandma stated. "It's about time you had one. And, of course, the right shoes will make all the difference in the world. Maybe we could put some lace around the neckline."

Sunshine thought of the beautiful old lace Pamela had sent. There was no way she was going to put that on this hideous dress. She wanted to cry, but she couldn't do that in front of Grandma. Somehow she managed to say, "Thanks, Grandma," and give her a hug.

After all, she meant well.

They decided that Sunshine would take all the dress parts and the rest of the material to her house, since it would be easier for the other girls to come there than to Grandma's. She was to get the measurements for Marybeth and Elena, then call Grandma to come over and help finish the other dresses.

When Sunshine got home, Mom said right away, "What's wrong?" She was standing at the kitchen counter, putting together some kind of sunflower seed and avocado salad for dinner. But she stopped what she was doing and turned to face Sunshine.

Wordlessly, Sunshine put the bundle she carried on the table, pulled out the dress, and held it up. "Grandma cut out the bridesmaids' dresses," she choked.

Brunhilda got up from her rug in the corner to come over and sniff the dress. She rejected it right away and returned to her rug.

Mom looked at the dress. "Oh, my," she whispered. "Oh, honey, I'm so sorry."

That was all it took to undo Sunshine's resolve not to cry. She totally lost it, breaking into sobs that shook her shoulders and hurt her chest.

Mom hurried over to put her arms around her, crushing the dress between them. Brunhilda came too, touching Sunshine's hand with her cold nose, apparently worried about the tears.

"I'm so sorry," Mom repeated. "Oh, I should have done something. I should have known better than to let you take the material over to her house."

"It's not your fault, Mom," Sunshine blubbered. "You didn't know."

"I know *her*," Mom said. "I should have guessed she'd go ahead with what *she* wanted. I lived with her for a long time, you know."

Sunshine let herself sob for a little while before she said, "Mom, I really do love Grandma."

"So do I," Mom murmured.

Sunshine snuffled back her tears. "But she's so . . . so . . . "

Mom patted her back. "I know. I guess none of us are perfect."

Sunshine pulled away to look at Mom. "But why would she do something like that? Why didn't she wait until I *told* her what pattern I wanted?"

Mom shook her head. "I don't know why she does the things she does."

Sunshine thought about that. She was beginning to understand why Mom was the way *she* was, rebellious and always going her own way even if sometimes she seemed a little odd. She'd probably got that way from being pushed around by Grandma.

So how had Grandma got to be the way *she* was?

"What was Grandma's mother like?" Sunshine asked.

Mom shook her head again. "She never would talk much about her." She took the dress from Sunshine. "Let's take a look at this now and see what we might do about it."

They both gazed at the dress.

"We'll think of something," Mom said, but she didn't sound very convincing.

Her tone reminded Sunshine of a verse from First Corinthians that Brother Dexter was always saying in their Sunday School class: "If the trumpet give an uncertain sound, who shall prepare himself to the battle?"

There wasn't even going to be a battle. Who could win over Grandma?

"Pamela's going to have a cow," Sunshine said glumly.

Brunhilda followed her into her bedroom and watched as she dropped the dress and the bundle with the other dress pieces and the rest of the material on her bed. She didn't care if the dress got wrinkled. Wrinkles couldn't make it any uglier.

The dog whined softly as Sunshine sat down at her desk and pulled her schoolbooks toward her.

"I know, Hildy," Sunshine said. "I know you want to play, but I don't feel like it. Life is the pits, isn't it?"

Brunhilda laid her head on Sunshine's knee.

Sunshine patted her. "You're going to have to wait for your walk. I've got to hit the books, thanks to Ducky's dad."

Brunhilda continued to gaze at her and wag her tail, whacking it against the desk.

"Okay, okay." Sunshine picked up the old tug-of-war towel the dog liked to play with and tossed it out for Brunhilda to grab in her mouth. She pulled then, and Brunhilda braced her feet and growled and shook her head.

After five minutes of play, Sunshine said, "Pack it in, dog. I have to work." She dropped her end of the towel.

Brunhilda continued to shake it, apparently sure it wasn't dead yet.

Sunshine opened her math book, but she couldn't concentrate. All she could think of was the ugly dress and the fact that the wedding was less than two weeks away.

Finally she gave up. "Let's go for that walk now, Hildy," she said.

That's how she and Brunhilda happened to be out on the street at the same time as Ducky and her dog were. They met at the corner of Mountain and Allen.

"I didn't know you had a dog," Sunshine said, looking at the shaggy mutt attached to the leash Ducky held. "What kind is he?"

"She," Ducky said. "She's a little bit of everything. She needed a home, so I didn't ask for her pedigree." She grinned at Sunshine. "What kind is yours?"

"Mom says she's a Baskin-Robbins," Sunshine said. "You know, thirty-one flavors?"

Suddenly it seemed as if she and Ducky had something in common. They both liked scroungy dogs.

"Her name's Sylvia," Ducky said. "I thought if I gave her a beautiful name, she'd think she was a beautiful dog."

Sunshine nodded. "This one's Brunhilda. Mom says that's a name from an opera. She's into operas."

She was curious about why Ducky didn't give *herself* a beautiful name, but she didn't ask about it.

But, of course, Ducky didn't need a beautiful name to think she was beautiful.

It reminded Sunshine that she had to pick a new name for herself to go in the newspaper articles on

Pamela's wedding. But it didn't matter much anymore. Her name was going to be Mud when the other girls saw what the bridesmaids' dresses were going to be like.

"Sylvia insisted I take her for a walk," Ducky was saying, "because I've been trying doggy duds on her all afternoon. I've got this idea to start a line of doggy coats, you know, like spoiled poodles wear when the temperature goes down to fifty degrees? So I've been using her for a model."

"Speaking of doggy duds," Sunshine started to say, thinking of the bridesmaid's dress. Suddenly she had an inspiration. Ducky was an expert on fashion and design. If anybody could figure out how to rescue the ugly peplum dress, she could.

"Ducky," she said, "I have a problem. Can you come to my house for a little while?"

CHAPTER 10

By the time they got to Sunshine's house, Sylvia and Brunhilda were friends. They wagged their tails and let their long pink tongues flop in and out. They growled playfully at each other. Once they were inside the yard with their leashes removed, they chased each other happily across the lawn.

"We'll just leave them out here while I show you what I need help with," Sunshine said.

She took Ducky inside and introduced her to her mother, who was sitting in their old wicker rocker, a treasure from yet another garage sale, reading something for her classes.

Mom and Ducky took to each other as fast as Sylvia and Brunhilda had done.

Ducky gazed around the little house and said, "I love this. Did you plan it all yourself?"

Mom laughed. "Who else? I call it Early Grunge decor."

Sunshine looked around her familiar house. She was so used to it that she hardly noticed anymore how it looked.

"It's delightful!" Ducky exclaimed. "I love all the bright colors and the homeliness." She clapped her hand over her mouth. "No, that's not what I mean. Not homeliness. *Homeyness* is what I meant to say."

Mom laughed again and said, "Let me show you a table I found last week at a garage sale. I'm sanding it down right now and then I'm going to . . . "

"Mom," Sunshine interrupted. "Ducky is here to help me with the dresses."

Mom's happy look faded away. "The dresses! I almost forgot them. Golly, Ducky, I hope you have some kind of inspiration, because I can't think what to do about them." She reached out to touch the top Ducky wore, made from gauzy, flowered material and styled with big, flowing sleeves. "Did you make this?"

Ducky nodded. "I make most of my clothes. I can't find anything in stores that I like as well as what I design in my own head."

Sunshine felt embarrassed that *she* had ever claimed to be a dress designer. Her designs were nowhere near as dramatic as Ducky's.

On the other hand, what she designed worked

well enough for *her.* There wasn't any reason why she should make the same designs as Ducky.

And if Ducky could figure out some way to make those ugly dresses look attractive, Sunshine could forgive her anything, even having more talent than anybody else in the world.

The two dogs, Sylvia and Brunhilda, came loping into the house as Sunshine led her mother and Ducky toward her room.

"Sylvia!" Ducky scolded. "You go on outside where you belong."

Sylvia tucked her tail between her legs and turned to go, but Sunshine put out a hand to pat her. "It's okay. Brunhilda is in the house most of the time. Let them stay."

Sunshine's small room was almost filled to capacity with three people and two dogs. Sunshine barely had enough room to hold up the dress Grandma had sewed.

Ducky stared at it for what seemed a long time.

"Oh, dear," she said finally.

"Yeah," Sunshine said.

Mom sighed loudly.

"I see what you mean," Ducky said.

"Any ideas?" Sunshine was still hopeful.

Slowly Ducky shook her head. She touched the

flared peplum of the dress. "How much material is there left?"

"Not enough for five more dresses," Sunshine said. "Grandma cut out three whole patterns." She picked up the package with the remaining material and unfolded it.

Ducky continued to shake her head. "There's not even enough there to do your candle dresses. You know, the design you showed us at McDonald's?"

Sunshine looked closely at Ducky to see if she was teasing her. But Ducky's face was serious.

"Maybe we could do knee-length straight dresses. They wouldn't be as pretty as the full-length ones, but they'd be better than this." Sunshine motioned toward the peplum dress. "There'd never be enough cloth left to do a design like Grandma's patchwork dress, the way we planned."

Ducky was quiet as she looked at the fabric.

In a corner of the room, the two dogs growled over the old towel Sunshine and Brunhilda played tug-of-war with. Each one had hold of an end, and they yanked and pulled on it, tearing it, playing happily together.

"Let me think about it," Ducky said finally. "When is the exact date of the wedding?"

"September 17. Two weeks away." Sunshine felt her heart pound with anxiety.

"Oh boy," Ducky said.

The phone rang and Mom went to answer it.

"Does the bride know the dresses aren't ready?" Ducky asked.

Sunshine shook her head.

"Oh boy," Ducky said again.

Mom came back into the room. "It's for you, Sunshine," she said. "It's Pamela. She came back from Idaho sooner than she'd expected."

Sunshine's heart pounded a little harder. "She probably wants to know about the dresses."

"She wants to see you," Mom said. "She's back here in Pasadena. She wants to meet with all of you."

"Oh boy," Sunshine groaned as she headed for the phone.

Pamela invited all of the girls in the Beehive class to come over to the new apartment where she and Jeff would live after their marriage.

Mom drove Sunshine and Ducky over there. Ducky worried all the way that she should have just taken Sylvia and gone home.

"She invited you too," Sunshine said. "She *said* you should come. And Sylvia is fine there at my house for a while."

Ducky worried aloud that she was horning in.

"She wants to talk about the wedding, and I'm not part of it."

"Yes, you are," Sunshine said. "You're going to help me figure out what to do about the dresses. That makes you part of it."

That made the worry lines deepen on Ducky's face. "What are you going to tell her about the dresses? Maybe she'll be expecting you to bring them for her to look at."

"She didn't say I should." Sunshine was worried about that too. Should she tell Pamela what a disaster they were? Or should she just bluff it out and trust that Ducky would come up with a new and wonderful design?

Mom went home after she dropped off the girls. "I'll go back and check on the dogs," she said. "Call me when you're finished."

The other girls were already there at the apartment, sitting on the floor and surrounded by enormous pillows.

"Sunshine!" Pamela exclaimed as she opened the door. "It's great to see you." She gave Sunshine a big hug.

"And you must be Ducky," she said, reaching out to take Ducky's hand. "I've heard a lot about you." She gave her a hug too.

"Jeff and I haven't had time to shop for furniture yet," she said, waving a hand around the empty room. "So we'll just have to go primitive and sit on the floor." She picked up two enormous pillows from a corner and handed them to Sunshine and Ducky. "I kind of like the pillow look anyway, don't you?"

Suddenly it was like the days when Pamela had been their teacher, when everything she suggested was fun. She was even prettier than before. She'd had her hair cut, which made her beautiful face show up even better. She was wearing peach-colored pants and a bright, flowered top, almost as colorful as Ducky's.

As soon as they were all on the floor, leaning on the big pillows, Pamela looked around at each face. "I can't tell you how much I've missed you," she said. "Nor how happy I am to meet you, Ducky. And the first thing I want to say, Ducky, is that I want you to be a bridesmaid too. Is there enough material for a dress for Ducky, Sunshine? I sent a little extra."

Sunshine gulped. What was she going to say? She was aware that Ducky was watching her.

"There's enough for a dress," she said.

Technically, that was no lie. There was uncut material for *two* dresses, but they were to be for Becca and Elena. But if Sunshine started explaining, then she'd have to tell about the peplum dresses.

"Good," Pamela said. "Will you do it, Ducky? Be a bridesmaid, I mean?"

"I'd love to," Ducky said.

Her face showed that she was very pleased to be asked, but Sunshine could see a little line of worry in her forehead. She knew Ducky too was wondering how they were going to make yet another of the ugly dresses out of what was left of the cloth.

"The maid-of-honor's dress is all ready," Pamela said. "Oh, let me show you my wedding dress."

She jumped up and ran into the bedroom, bringing back the lovely white dress, which had a full skirt, with the fitted bodice and high collar trimmed with the old lace from her great-grandmother's wedding dress.

The patchwork dress design would have been just perfect with Pamela's wedding gown. How was Sunshine ever going to tell her what had happened?

She *wasn't* going to tell her. She and Ducky would solve the problem somehow before Pamela had to see the dresses.

"The design of the maid-of-honor's dress is almost like this," Pamela was saying. "It's of the same material as your dresses, with insets of the background color."

Pamela took her gown back to the bedroom, then returned to tell the girls about how they were all to come over to the temple so that they'd be there when the ceremony was over. There would be a time for picture-taking on the temple grounds when she and Jeff and the guests who would witness the wedding came out, and she wanted the girls to be included in that.

Maybe she wouldn't want them included when she saw the dresses.

No, Sunshine decided. She had to stop thinking that way. She and Ducky were going to work miracles with the dresses. Maybe they could use the peplum material to make big collars or something so that nobody would notice that the skirts were so long and straight and skimpy.

Pamela went on telling them of all the things she and Jeff had to do before the big day. They had to find at least some of the furniture they needed, and they needed to meet with the caterers who would bring the food for the big reception. They had to figure out how they wanted the cultural hall decorated and then round up people to help them do it.

"I think we already talked about how I'd like you girls to circulate around, passing the hors d'oeuvres and taking care of the gifts," she said. "Is that still okay with you, or would you rather stand in the reception line?"

The girls looked at one another. "I'd rather circulate," Marybeth said.

"Me too," the others echoed.

Pamela nodded. "Good. That will cut down the length of the reception line. Besides Jeff and me, there'll be our parents and my maid-of-honor and Jeff's best man. That's enough of a line for people to shake hands with. And you girls will look so pretty, all dressed alike and weaving in and out through the crowd. Kind of tying it all together." She smiled.

Sunshine tried not to think about that. She concentrated instead on seeing herself pass a tray of delicious hors d'oeuvres to Arvy Dixon. She'd show him what real class was, not like him strutting around in a chicken suit.

He probably wouldn't even notice what she passed to him, since he'd be staring at her hideous dress.

There just wasn't any way she could avoid thinking about those dresses. No matter what she and Ducky did, the dresses were going to be a disaster.

At the end of the evening Pamela gave each girl a cup of hot chocolate and passed around some doughnuts she'd made herself. She said it was a recipe called Brother Brigham's Buttermilk Doughnuts that had been handed down through her family.

After they'd eaten and giggled together about

"the good old days" when Pamela had been their teacher, she drove them all home.

Sunshine's mother met Sunshine and Ducky at the door. "I didn't know whether to call Pamela's place or not," she said. Her face was pale.

"What's the matter?" Sunshine said. "What's happened?" Her heart began thudding again.

Mom seemed unable to say any more. "The dogs," she said, waving a hand toward Sunshine's room.

"Has something happened to Sylvia?" Ducky said in a scared voice. She ran toward Sunshine's room.

"The dogs are fine," Mom said. "They're in the backyard."

Ducky stopped in the doorway of Sunshine's room and gasped. Sunshine had to peer over her shoulder.

What she saw was scraps of cloth scattered all over the room.

For a moment she didn't know what it was. Then she saw that it was the length of dress material she'd left on the bed. It was torn into strips and pieces. The finished dress lay on the floor with its peplum pulled half off and the skirt shredded. The pattern pieces that Grandma had cut out were scattered all over the room, some of them totally ruined.

Obviously the dogs had played tug-of-war with whatever they found handy.

Sunshine's first emotion was relief. Relief that they wouldn't have to wear the peplum dresses anyway.

But then she realized that Pamela's beautiful material was destroyed.

"Oh, no!" she breathed. "Oh, *no!*"

She'd thought she had disaster on her hands before. But now! What was she going to do now?

CHAPTER
11

Sunshine felt so weak, she wondered if she might faint. Outside she could hear the two dogs, Brunhilda and Sylvia, barking and growling happily together.

How could they be so happy after they'd totally ruined Sunshine's life? Or at least her life in the immediate future? How was she going to tell the other Bee Theres that the bridesmaids' dresses were now nothing but strips and shreds of cloth?

How was she going to tell Pamela?

How much would it cost to buy an airplane ticket to Egypt, where she could hide out in the pyramids for a few dozen years?

Ducky walked into the bedroom and picked up what had been the long length of cloth that Grandma hadn't yet cut.

"There are parts of it that are still good," she said hopefully.

"Oh, sure." Sunshine picked up a piece of cloth that had been part of the finished dress. "There's enough good cloth left to make a hairbow for each of us."

Ducky's hopeful look faded, and Sunshine was sorry she'd spoken sharply. It wasn't Ducky's fault. Ducky had wanted to leave the dogs outside in the first place.

"I'm sorry," she said. "I guess I'm in shock."

Ducky nodded. "It's okay. Let's think about this now. There must be something we can do."

"We'll have to replace the material," Sunshine's mother said from the doorway.

But how could they replace it? Pamela had written that she'd looked for a long time to find exactly the right colors. It must have been expensive, too, because it was such lovely material.

Sunshine didn't have any money, except for maybe four dollars in the red candy box on her closet shelf. Why hadn't she saved her allowance for the past ten years instead of throwing it away on Big Macs and shakes at the Golden Arches?

Mom couldn't afford to pay for six dresses either. Unless she found them at a garage sale.

For just a moment Sunshine thought hopefully of

happening onto a garage sale where someone would be selling six beautiful bridesmaid dresses for a couple dollars each.

No way was that going to happen.

They had to match the maid-of-honor's dress anyway. Pamela had said that the maid-of-honor's dress was made of the same material as the bridesmaids' dresses.

So they'd just have to find more of the cloth.

"I'll get a job," Sunshine whispered.

"The wedding is just two weeks away," Ducky reminded her.

Sunshine groaned. "I'll work all night."

"Doing what?" Mom asked.

What *could* she do? She did babysitting sometimes, but people didn't usually need a babysitter except on weekends. That wouldn't bring in much money before the wedding.

How *did* people her age earn money? She thought of Arvy Dixon in his chicken suit, standing outside the Chicken Shack.

"I'll work at the Chicken Shack," she said. "Arvy said they needed somebody during the hours he couldn't be there."

"Which are the same hours *you* can't be there," Mom said. "You're not going to ditch school for this, you know."

"Look," Ducky said. "Let's do this." She held up a scrap of the material. "Let's each take a piece of this and go around to all the different fabric shops in the area to see if we can match it. If we can, then at least we can find out how much it's going to cost to replace."

Sunshine ran a finger over the pretty material. "And if we can't find a match?"

"Then we'll figure out the next step," Ducky said. "I'll call my mom to come get me and take me to Fashion Park."

Sunshine's mom headed toward the living room. "Let me get my car keys, Sunshine, and I'll take you to the Plaza Mall. There are fabric shops there."

"I'll call the other Bee Theres," Sunshine said. She was beginning to feel as if there might be some hope. "Maybe some of them could go over to the Galleria and the Eagle Rock Mall to check things out."

Ducky looked at her. "Bee Theres? What's that?"

Sunshine's face reddened a little when she remembered that they hadn't told Ducky about the Bee Theres.

"Oh," she said as if it wasn't much of anything, "it's just a little club we have."

"Maybe they won't want to come," Ducky said.

Sunshine wondered how much she should tell

Ducky. Wouldn't Ducky wonder why they hadn't invited her to join?

This wasn't the time to worry about that. "They'll come," Sunshine said. "That's what the club is all about, that we'll always 'be there' for one another."

Ducky nodded slowly, but all she said was, "Let me call my mom first, then you call the troops." She headed for the telephone in the hall.

"We'll meet at McDonald's to report," Sunshine called after her before stooping down to gather up the scraps of material and stack them on the bed. She selected several pieces that weren't too torn so she could give one to each girl as a sample.

They just *had* to find matching material.

Ducky's mom came and picked up her and Sylvia. They were going to leave Sylvia off at home, then head straight to Fashion Park.

Two other mothers were available to drive their daughters around to the malls. Becca's mom was teaching a class at the university where she worked, and Elena's mom was taking Elena's younger brothers for a dental checkup. So Becca went with Carlie and her mom, and Elena rode along with Marybeth and her mom. The girls worked out a plan to cover all the fabric stores within the area.

Sunshine and her mom were almost to the freeway entrance when they saw Arvy Dixon riding along the street on his bicycle.

"Stop, Mom," Sunshine said. "Please."

Mom looked a little puzzled, but she pulled over to the curb.

"Arvy," Sunshine called, opening the car door and getting out.

Arvy looked surprised that she would call out to him, and he even blushed a little as he rode up to the car.

"Hi," he said. He leaned over and looked inside the car. "Hi, Mrs. McGee."

Sunshine knew Mom would probably say what a nice boy Arvy was as soon as they started off again. She shoved that thought aside and asked, "Arvy, how many chicken suits does the Chicken Shack have?"

Arvy thought about it. "Six. There's only me and Jamahl that use them right now." He looked closely at Sunshine. "Why?" Sunshine was thinking of the six chicken suits. One for each of the Beehive girls. How long would it take to earn the money for the new material if they all got jobs at the Chicken Shack?

"We need six bridesmaids' outfits for Pamela's wedding," she said. If each girl earned enough money for one dress by standing on the street dressed in a chicken suit and carrying the Chicken Shack sign, they'd be able to pay for the new material. If they *found* some new material.

Arvy nodded. "I'll see when the suits might be available," he said. "When do you want them?"

"As soon as possible." Sunshine was thinking about what hours the girls might work. Maybe they'd just have to neglect all that homework they'd been assigned.

"Okay." Arvy seemed happy that he could help.

"Thanks," Sunshine said, getting back into the car.

She glanced back once as Mom drove up the freeway ramp. Arvy stood watching them go.

He was nice.

Maybe one of these days he'd even quit chanting "Buzzy little Beehives" or singing "There is sunshine in my soul today" when he saw her and the other girls.

Or maybe that was the way he showed how he felt about her. She remembered how her great-grandmother had written that when Harvey yanked her hair, she knew he loved her.

Boys were hard to understand.

Sunshine and her mother searched through every fabric store in Pasadena, but found nothing that matched the material Pamela had sent for the dresses. They didn't even find anything remotely similar.

In one store Mom held up some pretty flowered cloth patterned with pale orange and yellow flowers against a brown background. "This is the closest we've seen," she said. "Do you think it might do?"

Sunshine shook her head. "It has to be the same as in the maid-of-honor's dress."

Mom put the material down. Taking the sample scrap of cloth Sunshine had brought with her, she found the store manager and asked if there was any way she could find material like that.

"Do you know the manufacturer?" the manager asked. "And the dye lot?"

Mom shook her head.

The manager looked as if she wanted to be help-ful. "Where did you buy this?"

Mom explained how Pamela had bought it in Idaho.

"The best thing to do then," the manager said, "is to send the sample to the store and ask if they still have some or if they could order some specially for you. It would take a while, but they could probably get it eventually."

Mom looked at Sunshine. "That's what we'll have to do." She thanked the store manager, and they headed for the car.

"We'll have to tell Pamela what happened," Mom said. "We can have the store send the new material by overnight mail."

"*If* they've got it," Sunshine said. "There isn't time to order any if they don't already have it."

The meeting at McDonald's after the mothers dropped the girls off was gloomy. Nobody had found any matching material.

They all ordered hamburgers and fries, but nobody ate much.

Sunshine told them what the store manager had said about contacting the store in Idaho. "But we'll have to tell Pamela." The other girls groaned.

"She's going to think I'm a total idiot," Sunshine said.

"She's going to think we're *all* total idiots," Marybeth said.

"It'll ruin her wedding," Elena said.

"It'll probably ruin her whole *life*," Carlie said.

Sunshine had a new thought. "She'll probably say she doesn't need six bridesmaids, when we tell her. She has so many things to worry about right now that she'll say she can't handle this and just cancel us."

Ducky slapped a hand on the table. "Hey, look, you guys," she said. "Pamela would understand, if we tell her. But let's not rush into anything. Let's go back to Sunshine's house and see how much of the cloth is still usable. Maybe we can figure something out."

She held up the scrap of cloth she'd taken with her. "There's still enough material for headbands. Or bows for our shoulders. Or sashes. Or even scarves to cover our eyes so we won't see Pamela's reaction."

She grinned.

"Come on now," she said. "Trust me. We'll work something out. Like I said, I'm used to making swans out of ugly ducklings."

Okay. Let her take it over. Sunshine gave up.

CHAPTER
12

They'd no sooner arrived at Sunshine's house than there was a knock at the door.

"Excuse me," Sunshine said. "It's probably a vacuum cleaner salesman. I'll tell him to get lost."

She opened the door, ready to tell the knocker she didn't want any of whatever it was he was selling. But it was no vacuum cleaner salesman standing on the porch. It was Pamela and her fiancé, Jeff, tall and resplendent in his copilot's uniform.

"Oh," Sunshine said. Was Pamela there to see the bridesmaids' dresses? Would she yell at Sunshine when she found out what was going on? What was Jeff going to think about the disaster?

"Hi, Sunshine," Pamela said. "Marybeth's mother told us you'd probably be coming here when you finished eating at McDonald's. I'm glad we caught you.

121

Jeff just got in from a flight, and he's helping me with some of the jillion things I have to do."

"Oh," Sunshine said again. "Oh, *Pamela. Jeff!* Come in!"

She turned toward the other girls and said, "It's Pamela and Jeff." As if they couldn't see well enough with their own eyes who it was.

The other girls ran over to hug Pamela. Even Ducky hugged her, thanking her again for letting her be a bridesmaid when she'd barely met her.

Pamela introduced them all to Jeff. They were a little shy around him since he was so impressive, standing there in his dark blue uniform.

"Hi, little Bees," he said. "Don't I get in on the hugs? Have you forgotten all those letters you wrote to me at your sleep-overs?"

Pamela used to have them write the letters because she said she wanted him to get acquainted with her "Bees."

Shyly each of the Bee Theres hugged him around the waist. When it was Ducky's turn, she said, "I'm Ducky. I haven't written any letters to you, but I'm going to hug you anyway."

Jeff laughed as Ducky wrapped her arms around his waist.

She'd probably become *his* favorite too. *Everybody* liked Ducky.

So what did it matter? The *big* problem was what to say if Pamela asked about the dresses. Sunshine hated to look like a total fud right there in front of Jeff. He wasn't the kind who made mistakes. People who made hideous mistakes couldn't fly huge airplanes with hundreds of lives depending on them.

"Won't you sit down?" Sunshine asked when all the hugs were over.

Pamela shook her head. "We don't really have time. I just wanted to check things out with you." She rummaged around in the shoulder bag she carried and pulled out a sheet of paper. "I'm getting the wedding announcement ready to submit to the newspaper so it can come out right after the Big Day. I want to make sure I have everything correct."

She began reading off names. "Becca Martin," she said. "It's not Rebecca, as I recall. Just Becca."

"Right," Becca said.

Pamela continued. "Marybeth Stewart. Carlie Kuramoto. Elena Perez. Sunshine McGee. And Ducky . . . " She looked at Ducky. "Is that your given name or a nickname?"

Ducky smiled. "It's the name I use."

"Would you like me to use your real name in the article?"

Ducky shook her head. "Just use Ducky. Ducky Dumont. D-U-M-O-N-T."

Pamela looked as if she wanted to know what Ducky's real name was as much as the Bee Theres did. But she didn't ask. She was too polite for that.

Sunshine wondered if they'd ever find out what Ducky's real name was.

"Okay." Pamela consulted the typed page she held. "Now, the last thing I need is a description of the bridesmaids' dresses. I'm going to say that they were designed by you, Sunshine."

Oh, wow. Sunshine wished she'd picked a new name for herself so that nobody who read the article would know who it was who designed the dresses. *If* the dresses ever got made. Maybe there was still time to pick a new name. Ophelia maybe? She was the poor girl who drowned in a brook in that Shakespeare play Mom had taken her to see last summer. Or Charlotte? The spider who died? Either would be appropriate, since die was what Sunshine was going to do if the dresses didn't work out.

"Do you have to send in the article right now?" she said.

"No." Pamela folded the sheet of paper and put it inside her purse. "I don't have to submit it yet. Why?"

"Well, uh, uh . . . , " Sunshine stammered.

"But I really need to start writing a description of the dresses for the article," she explained. "Could I see one of them?"

Sunshine felt she was going to choke. She could see the eyes of the other girls get big.

"The dresses aren't here," Ducky said smoothly. "Can we show them to you in a few days?"

"They're going to be a big surprise," Carlie said. That was no lie!

"Okay," Pamela said agreeably. "Let me know as soon as you can." She turned to Jeff. "I guess we'd better rush off now. We have several other errands to run."

Sunshine walked to the door with them, but when she opened it she saw Arvy and Jamahl standing on the porch. Arvy's arms were piled high with something yellow and feathery. Chicken suits from the Buck-a-Cluck Chicken Shack. Jamahl carried an enormous bag from which a big chicken foot protruded.

"Hi," Arvy said. "I was just going to knock."

Sunshine stared at them. Why were they coming to her house? "We brought your bridesmaids' outfits," Arvy said. He held up his yellow armful.

Sunshine was horrified as Pamela stepped forward to look at what Arvy carried.

"Well, aren't you the sly ones," Pamela said, "letting me worry that the outfits weren't finished. Now I can finish my article."

She took one of the suits from Arvy and held it up.

She didn't say anything.

Jeff fished a pair of chicken feet from Jamahl's huge bag.

He didn't say anything either.

Sunshine felt as if she were choking. Why had Arvy done this?

It was Jeff who finally spoke. "You're going to be chickens at our wedding reception?" He looked around at all of the girls. "*Chickens?*"

"No," Sunshine whispered. She glared at Arvy. "Why did you bring this stuff here?"

Arvy looked bewildered. "But you *said*. Yesterday. You *said*."

Sunshine tried to remember what she'd said.

"*You* know," Arvy prompted. "You asked how many chicken outfits there were, and I said six. *You* said you needed six bridesmaids' outfits, and *I* said I'd see if the suits were available."

"I *didn't* say I wanted them for bridesmaids' outfits," Sunshine said. "I just meant . . . "

She couldn't say right there in front of Pamela and Jeff that she was asking about the suits because she and the other girls needed to work at the Buck-a-Cluck Chicken Shack to earn money to buy new material for the bridesmaids' dresses. She couldn't add to Pamela's worries by letting her know there might not *be* any bridesmaids' dresses.

"I mean, that wasn't what I meant," she said finally.

Pamela and Jeff were watching her suspiciously. The other girls looked horrified.

"Sunshine," Pamela said. "I remember how you always liked to play jokes on the rest of us. You weren't really going to come to my wedding reception as chickens, were you?"

Sunshine's face burned. "Pamela, no. I wouldn't do anything like that." She felt like crying.

Pamela looked at her for a moment before she smiled. "Oh, I know you wouldn't. But I'm really getting a little worried now. Where is the material I sent for the dresses?"

"It's here," Sunshine said miserably. She thought of the piles of shredded cloth in her bedroom.

Pamela raised her eyebrows. "But Ducky said the dresses aren't here."

"The *dresses* aren't here," Sunshine said.

Pamela frowned. "I don't understand."

Ducky moved forward. "Pamela," she said. "Think of your wedding dress. Think of how the skirt is draped around to the back to sweep majestically to the floor as you walk."

Ducky paraded in front of Pamela and Jeff, looking behind her as if to watch a majestically draped skirt.

"Now think of the fitted long sleeves," she said, "enhanced with lace from your grandmother's wedding dress, which cunningly draws the generations together."

She sounded like the commentator of the fashion show that had been the program for a Mother-Daughter night last fall. Ducky had certainly been in enough fashion shows to know how they talked. She was making them see Pamela's wedding dress when it wasn't even there.

"Now," Ducky continued, "think of the bodice, rising like an opening tulip from the nipped-in waist to the high lace collar, enhanced by your mother's cameo, thus again reminding the viewer of the steady progression of generations."

Ducky had made up the part about the cameo, but it sounded good. Sunshine was impressed.

So was Pamela. Her eyes looked a little misty as she watched Ducky.

Jeff was another matter. His eyes were slightly narrowed as he watched Ducky.

"Now," Ducky said, "think of the six bridesmaids' dresses, reflecting the design of your wedding dress but each with its own individuality. Each wearer with her own personality expressed. Each one adding to the overall picture of a joyous, happy bride and groom."

Ducky strutted before them all, making them almost believe that the bridesmaids' dresses were going to be magnificent.

Arvy and Jamahl, still standing there loaded with chicken suits, appeared to be totally enchanted. Jamahl, especially. His eyes glazed over and his mouth hung open as he watched Ducky.

"Wow," he said when she finished her little parade with a flourish and smiled at her audience.

Pamela looked slightly relieved. "Well, I don't know what's going on, and I don't know why this all has to be such a secret, but I trust you girls completely. I'll just leave it in your hands and be pleasantly surprised. I hope." She took Jeff's arm. "But no chickens."

As they left, Jeff turned around and gave Ducky a big wink.

"Great snow job," he whispered.

The girls watched them get inside Jeff's car and drive away before anybody spoke.

Then Becca turned to Ducky. "You sure saved our necks," she said. "But we're still right back in Disaster City."

"Maybe not," Sunshine said. She smiled at Ducky. "That was quite a show. It gave me an idea about what we might do."

She wasn't at all sure it would work. But it was their last chance.

The other girls waited for Sunshine to say something further. But suddenly she felt shy about her idea. She wished she could experiment with it first, make at least one dress and try it on before she showed the others.

"Well," Becca said. "Tell."

Sunshine cleared her throat. "Uh . . . " Nervously she twisted her lock of purple hair.

"Say it," Elena urged.

"Patchwork dresses," Sunshine blurted.

Carlie nodded. "We already approved your grandmother's patchwork dress design. So what's your idea?"

"That's it. Patchwork bridesmaids' dresses," Sunshine repeated. "We don't have enough of the original material to make six dresses. But we have enough to make a lot of big patches."

The other girls looked puzzled.

"It might work." Sunshine was beginning to feel desperate. "We'll make squares from what Pamela sent us. Then we can cut up any other good material we can find. We can bring skirts and other things that we don't wear anymore but that are still good. We'll cut big patches out of them too."

Becca, Carlie, Elena, and Marybeth frowned. Arvy and Jamahl stared at Sunshine with "Huh?" looks on their faces.

"Do you think Pamela will like that?" Carlie asked. "Maybe we'd better tell her."

Sunshine shook her head. "If she hates it, her day will be ruined. But it's too late to figure out anything else, so let's surprise her, like we said. She won't see us until she and Jeff come out of the temple, and by then she's at least had a beautiful wedding ceremony."

"We'll look like a whole bunch of patchwork quilts," Marybeth said gloomily.

Well, so it wasn't a good idea after all. Sunshine wished she hadn't even suggested it.

"Hey, no, listen," Ducky said suddenly. "I think it's terrific. What we can do is make panels of the original material, and then fill in between with odds and ends."

"Odds and ends?" Elena's voice dripped doubt.

"Look around you," Ducky said. "Look at what Sunshine and her mother have done with odds and ends and pieces of furniture and rugs that they've found at garage sales. Look how they've painted things to coordinate with other things, and picked up the colors in the curtains and rugs."

The girls looked around.

"I've always loved your house," Marybeth said.

Marybeth loved it? Sunshine could hardly believe her ears. Marybeth lived in a big, two-story house that had been professionally decorated. But she loved Sunshine's little patchwork house!

The others nodded. "Me too," they each said.

"Well," Ducky said, "we can do the same thing with the dresses."

Sunshine wasn't quite sure just how the two things were similar, and she could see that the other girls still had doubts.

"I'll do makeup for all of us," Ducky offered. "Just a little to accent our eyes and stuff. But not enough so our moms will freak out. That way we'll be so gorgeous nobody will notice what we're wearing."

"Yes!" Becca said, and the others repeated, "YES!"

Now the girls were all smiling and nodding.

Sunshine was majorly grateful to Ducky, who'd been the one to get them to agree, although she was pretty sure it was the makeup, not the patchwork idea, that they were yessing.

"We'll all contribute some kind of cloth for the dresses," Marybeth said.

Arvy Dixon suddenly went into action. He laid all of the chicken suits he'd been holding on the sofa. From the inside of one costume's leg he pulled a couple of the short strips of cloth that were supposed to resemble feathers.

"Here," he said. "Nobody will ever miss a few pieces of these chicken suits. Jamahl and I want to make a contribution to the dresses too."

Jamahl grinned. "How about matching footwear?" He motioned toward the big bag of yellow chicken feet he held.

Everybody laughed. The mood had changed completely from the despair they'd all felt a few minutes before.

But the big question remained: Would Pamela like the patchwork bridesmaids' dresses?

Grandma wasn't so easy to convince as the girls were. When Sunshine finished telling her about the cloth disaster and about what they were going to do about it, she said, "Patchwork? And makeup on twelve-year-old girls? What are people going to say?"

She also fussed again about Sunshine's lock of purple hair. "You've got to get that washed out, or they'll be talking about you all over town," she said.

"Who's 'they,' Grandma?" Sunshine asked.

Grandma harrumphed a couple of times before she said, "People. People in the ward. Pamela's friends."

"One of Pamela's friends has spiked orange hair and a nose ring, Grandma."

Grandma's face flushed. "Are you trying to aggravate me, young lady?"

Sunshine didn't want to upset Grandma. But she liked her lock of purple hair, although it hadn't changed a thing. Ducky was still the one who got noticed, mainly because besides being beautiful, she seemed able to do anything. She really could, as she'd said once, make swans out of ugly ducklings.

"I'm sorry, Grandma," Sunshine said.

"Well," Grandma grumped, "I guess my bridesmaid's dress pattern won't do anymore. So let's go look in my trunk and see if there is some material you can use for your patches." She said "patches" as if the word tasted bad.

For the next week the girls met at Sunshine's house every day after school. They cut hundreds of squares and pinned them together to see how they coordinated. They sewed long strips of them together. It took a lot of time.

It was a hard week because the teachers at school, inspired by Ducky's dad, the principal, were piling on the homework. Sometimes the girls wondered if they would get all of the dresses ready in time.

Sunshine's grandma came to help, most days. It was her suggestion that they see if they had enough of Pamela's material to cut six bodices so that only the skirts would be patchwork. She spent a long time fitting the pattern they'd made onto the larger pieces of cloth, trying it this way and that, to make use of every inch.

It worked. She was able to cut out six bodices and twelve short, slightly puffed sleeves.

While Grandma was doing that, Sunshine and Ducky made long, thin panels from what was left of Pamela's material and from some lovely pale peach material that had been in Grandma's trunk.

Then it was time to make the first dress. Grandma offered to do it. She fed the pieces into her whirring sewing machine, doing a tidy zigzag stitch around each square of patchwork.

Ducky modeled the finished dress, strutting around Sunshine's living room as if she were on a models' runway.

"It's gorgeous," Elena and Marybeth said in unison.

And it was. The warm colors glowed. The skirt, which Grandma had insisted on lining with some acetate material she'd found in her trunk, rustled as Ducky moved. The collar, edged with the lace from Pamela's great-grandmother, gave the dress an old-fashioned look.

"There's a piece of the skirt I wore at my eighth birthday party," Elena said, pointing.

Becca reached out to touch a piece of gold-colored material. "Here's a piece of my roadshow costume."

There were also some scraps left over from matching skirts Pamela had helped the girls make when she'd first been their teacher.

"And I see pieces of Arvy and Jamahl's chicken suits," Carlie said.

It was true. Ducky had cut the yellow chicken suit material into small triangles and then patched them into the corners of several squares for each dress.

They were all represented there, all pulled together with a little ingenuity, to make a lovely dress.

How could Pamela *not* like dresses like that?

Pamela called on Monday of the last week before the wedding, saying she had to have a description of what they were going to wear, for the newspaper article. Ducky talked to her, managing to describe the dresses without saying a word about patchwork. She reminded Pamela that they'd been designed by Sunshine, which made Sunshine wish again that she'd had time to pick a new name, if only to disguise herself.

Pamela also asked if they wanted to come to the wedding luncheon at a big restaurant or if they'd rather that she pay their bill at the nearest McDonald's.

They didn't even have to vote on that one.

"McDonald's," Ducky told her after a brief consultation with the others.

Pamela laughed. "I thought so."

On the morning of the wedding, the girls met at Sunshine's house to get ready. Grandma came over early to put the last-minute finishing touches on the dresses. She brought Sunshine a bra.

"Heaven knows you don't need it," she said in her usual candid way, "but I thought you'd feel more grown up if you were wearing one."

Sunshine was delighted. There wasn't much to the bra, but she'd been wanting to get one. She knew that Ducky must already wear one, and she suspected Becca did, although they hadn't ever discussed it.

Grandma sat down immediately to finish the dresses. Each one was different from the others, since they were all made up of a different arrangement of patches. But they were all lovely, the girls agreed when they came and tried them on.

Pamela and Jeff were being married at eleven o'clock, and everybody who didn't go with them to the temple was supposed to be at the ornate back door at noon. That's where they'd be coming out for pictures.

Ducky brought her makeup kit to Sunshine's house. It was a big gray case filled with tubes and boxes and jars. The girls handled the stuff, wanting to experiment. But there wasn't time.

Ducky started with Sunshine and did the whole works, beginning with cleansing cream, followed by foundation, then blusher and eye liner and mascara. Lipstick and a light dusting of powder finished the job.

Sunshine was disappointed when she looked into the mirror. She'd expected some great, dramatic change. She'd expected a swan, but she looked much the same as always, except that her eyelids looked a little smudged. She wasn't exactly an ugly duckling, but she was still Sunshine. Tapioca-pudding Sunshine.

It made her feel a little better when Grandma

threw up her hands and said, "You're not going out like that, are you?"

She guessed something showed.

Ducky made up the other girls, and Becca did everybody's hair in French braids intertwined with peach-colored ribbon and just a sprig of a delicate flower that Grandma called baby's breath.

Becca's mother drove them the thirty-five miles to the temple in her minivan. There wasn't room for any of the other mothers. Besides, Sunshine's and Carlie's moms were both at the church, helping to set up tables and get things ready for the reception that night.

The girls wore their usual clothes and stopped at the home of one of Pamela's friends near the temple to change. Since disasters seemed to be in the air, they didn't want to take any chances.

Before they could scarcely realize it, they were there at the temple, waiting by the big back door.

Sunshine was still a little nervous, even though she knew they all looked pretty in their patchwork outfits.

They *didn't* look like so many patchwork quilts. Did they?

No, they looked terrific. And in the bright sun-light, you could even tell that they wore makeup, which made Sunshine suddenly feel beautiful as she walked around in her rustling skirt.

They watched another bride and groom come out of the temple and pose with their family and attendants on the steps.

Then it was Pamela and Jeff's turn.

"Here they are," somebody announced.

And there was Pamela, looking so beautiful in a cloud of white that Sunshine's breath caught in her throat. Jeff, in a gray tuxedo, walked beside her, holding her hand.

They waved to everybody as they came out, then looked at each other, their faces reflecting the happiness they felt.

Flashbulbs went off. The official photographer yelled instructions. "I want all the attendants to come up and stand with them on the stairs," he said. "Then we'll get some pictures under the trees."

The maid-of-honor and best man were already there on the stairs. The maid-of-honor's dress was mostly solid peach-colored, made of the fabric she'd sent to the Bee Theres, with insets in a different shade. It almost had a patchwork look to it, Sunshine decided.

Pamela looked out over the crowd. "Where are my little Bees?"

"Here we are," Marybeth said, putting up her

hand. The girls moved forward, the crowd parting to let them through.

"This is it," Becca whispered. "Now we'll see how she likes our surprise."

Pamela smiled brightly as she caught sight of them. Then, as they moved together up the stairs, her face crumpled and she burst into tears.

CHAPTER
14

The six girls stopped, all in a clump. They stood close together, as if to draw strength from one another.

Pamela was crying! She hated the patchwork dresses!

"Oh, Pamela," Sunshine started to say. She was going to tell Pamela and everybody else that it was all her fault. She was the one who'd left the fabric for the dresses where the dogs could get at it. She was the one who'd thought up the stupid patchwork idea.

But before she could say any of it, the sweating photographer directed all six girls to line up to the left of the maid-of-honor.

Miserably they lined up.

There were more instructions as the photographer rearranged them so that they were in the order of their height, Ducky first, then Marybeth, Sunshine, Elena, Becca, and Carlie.

Jeff pulled a big white handkerchief from his pocket and handed it to Pamela, who dabbed at her face, drying her eyes while the photographer looked through his camera. She looked over at the brides-maids a couple of times, and once she tried to come over to them, but the photographer told her to stay where she was.

"She was probably going to tell us to go home," Becca muttered.

"Stop talking," the photographer yelled. "We have only a few minutes until the next bride and groom come out. Now smile."

The Bee Theres smiled.

"Wait," Pamela said. She gave the handkerchief back to Jeff. "Okay, I'm ready now."

The Bee Theres kept smiling. The photographer flashed a few pictures, then told the girls to stand on the steps behind the bride and groom. He probably wanted to cover up as much as he could of the dresses.

After several more flashes, the entire party was directed to stand in front of one of the beautiful beds of flowers. Pamela tried to come over to the girls again, but somebody grabbed her to adjust her veil.

After that it was chaos, with people pushing them all into different poses and flashbulbs going off.

Eventually the photographer said he was through with the attendants but that he wanted to take more pictures of just the bride and groom. Everybody else could go, if they wanted to.

At one point Pamela managed to say, "I'll talk to you later," to the girls, but then she was swept along to another spot for pictures.

"She's going to tell us not to come to the reception," Becca said gloomily.

They all thought about that. Ducky shook her head.

"If she hated the dresses that much," she said, "she would have told us not to be in the pictures at all."

That didn't cheer Becca up. "She tried. But the photographer didn't give her a chance."

The girls headed back to Becca's mother's minivan. Sunshine was really grateful now that they'd chosen to go to McDonald's for lunch rather than to the wedding luncheon at a restaurant near the temple. At least Pamela wouldn't have to look at the dresses for the next two hours.

And that night at the reception? Well, they would be running around serving hors d'oeuvres and stashing gifts in the Relief Society room, so maybe they could just stay out of Pamela's sight.

Or maybe they should just stay home. Maybe that really was what Pamela had tried to tell them.

After they went back to Pamela's friend's house to change out of the patchwork dresses, Becca's mother found a McDonald's. The tables were big enough for only six, so she took her lunch and went outside—"to enjoy the sunshine," she told them.

"Even *she* doesn't want to be seen with us," Marybeth whispered.

"That's not it," Becca said. "She's studying up for a new class she's teaching this fall at the university. She always brings her books with her, wherever she goes."

It was just as well that she didn't sit with them, because they needed to talk.

"I'll tell Pamela the patchwork dresses were my fault," Sunshine said after they got their food. "I'll tell her she doesn't need to be mad at the rest of you."

Ducky shook her head. "No, no. It's my fault. I was the one who kept on it after you said we should forget it. *I'm* the one to blame. She doesn't know me very well, so it doesn't matter as much if she's mad at me."

When the other girls opened their mouths to object, she said, "That's the way it's going to be. I insist."

Marybeth tapped her hand on the table to get

everybody's attention. "Now listen to your president, you guys. We're all in this together. We'll face it together. After all, we're the Bee Theres, aren't we?"

"I'm not," Ducky said.

Marybeth looked at the other girls and raised her eyebrows. Sunshine knew what she was asking. Should they invite Ducky to be a member of their club? That would mean that as long as they were all together, Ducky would be setting a high standard in everything they did. It sounded exhausting.

On the other hand, there was no way they were going to abandon Ducky to take the blame for the patchwork dresses. Besides, Sunshine knew they all wanted Ducky in the club anyway.

Everyone nodded.

"All in favor of sustaining Ducky as a member of the Bee Theres Club, please indicate by the uplifted hand," Marybeth said, sounding just like Bishop Tolman.

She, Elena, Becca, Carlie, and Sunshine all raised their right hands.

"So," Marybeth said, "you are now officially a Bee There, Ducky."

"On one condition," Sunshine said.

They all looked at her, puzzled.

"On the condition that you tell us what your real name is," Sunshine said.

Grinning, Ducky stood up and bowed. "I accept membership in the Bee Theres." She sat back down. "And I'll tell you my real name, but if you ever breathe it to another person, I'll work up some of my conjure-woman ancestor's magic and I'll turn you all into chickens. And not just costume chickens, like Arvy and Jamahl."

The girls leaned closer. "What is it?" Carlie whispered.

Ducky looked to the left, then to the right, as if to see if anyone was listening. Then she whispered, "I'll tell you tonight at the stroke of midnight in the church parking lot under the old pine tree."

The girls laughed in anticipation, and for just a few minutes they forgot about the dress disaster.

Grandma was at still the house when Sunshine got home.

"How did everything go?" she asked.

Sunshine wondered how much she should tell her. Why had Grandma let them go ahead with a dumb idea like patchwork dresses? Even her maroon peplum dress would have been better.

But it wasn't Grandma's fault. She'd just gone along with the idea when Sunshine said that's what they were doing.

"Oh, Grandma," she said, "Pamela hated the dresses."

Grandma looked startled. "Hated them? That's impossible, Sunshine. No, she might have hated that purple mess in your hair, but the dresses? No way, José."

Sunshine had never heard Grandma use slang before. She didn't even know Grandma *knew* any slang. It lowered her resistance, and suddenly she was sobbing in Grandma's arms, telling her everything that had happened.

"What are we going to do, Grandma?" she said when she could speak.

Grandma pulled one of her cedar-scented hankies from a pocket and wiped Sunshine's face as if she were a little kid. "Do?" she said. "You're going to put on those dresses and go do what Pamela asked you to do. The dresses are lovely, but not nearly as beautiful as the girls who will be wearing them. That's what made Pamela cry, Sunshine."

Sunshine wasn't used to hearing praise from Grandma. She was surprised to realize that Grandma had patches in her personality that Sunshine hadn't even realized were there. There were big pieces of her that were critical and bossy, but apparently there were others that were warm and loyal and loving.

"I love you, Grandma," Sunshine said.

* * * * *

There was total chaos in the cultural hall at the church when Sunshine and the other Bee Theres arrived. They had come early for more pictures, and the caterers were still piling food on the tables. There were a dozen big round tables in the hall, all covered with peach-colored cloths. Somebody was rearranging the rented potted palms that had been brought in for decoration, and somebody else was fussing with a white lattice thing that Pamela and Jeff were going to stand in front of. A band was getting set up on a riser in a corner of the hall.

"Come get your flowers," the maid-of-honor called to the Bee Theres. "You're to have bouquets for the pictures."

She pulled small bouquets of flowers from a big flat box and handed one to each of the girls.

Then there were pictures in front of the lattice-work thing, and outside, and in one of the rooms with all of the attendants pretending to help Pamela put a blue garter on one leg just below the knee. Throughout it all there was the soft rustle of skirts and the scent and sight of the autumn-colored flowers.

If it hadn't been for the worry about the dresses, Sunshine would have said it was the most exciting moment of her life, so far. She hoped that someday she could have a wedding just like Pamela's.

But probably without patchwork bridesmaids' dresses.

Pamela hadn't said anything about the dresses. Of course, she hadn't had the opportunity yet, since somebody had been posing her here or there ever since the Bee Theres had arrived.

Or was she deliberately ignoring them?

But she had smiled at them a couple of times.

Suddenly somebody was yelling, "Pamela! Jeff! You've got to form the reception line. People are starting to come in."

It was then that Pamela, in her cloud of white, floated over to the Bee Theres and said, "I've changed my mind. I want you girls to stand in the line with us for a while. So what if it's too long?" She tried to hug the whole group.

Sunshine almost choked. "You want us in the line?"

"Absolutely," Pamela said. "I want everybody to see these wonderful dresses my little Bees have created."

"You *like* them?" Becca gasped.

"I *love* them," Pamela said. "I loved them the minute I saw them. And when I saw you'd even included patches from those skirts we made last year, I cried. There are bits and pieces of our lives in those dresses. And you've brought them all together for this big moment in my life." She reached out to Carlie's dress and touched a panel of the fabric she'd sent. Her voice wobbled as she said, "I love you kids."

They had only a moment to cry together before Pamela was whisked away to stand by Jeff's side. Somebody showed the six girls where they should stand, and then people started coming down the line, laughing, shaking hands, saying how beautiful everybody looked.

And suddenly Sunshine felt beautiful. When Arvy Dixon came down the line, stammering out his congratulations to the bride and groom and turning totally tongue-tied when he came to the Bee Theres, she gave him a smile that made him blush.

It made her wonder how big of a patch he was going to be in the fabric of her life.

The reception didn't last until midnight, but Ducky told the other Bee Theres her real name out in the parking lot by the old pine tree as soon as Pamela and Jeff left in the midst of a shower of rice.

"It's Marian," Ducky whispered, as if she didn't want anybody else to hear.

There was a small silence while the other girls thought about the name. Marian.

"It's a pretty name," Sunshine said. "Why don't you want anybody to know?"

"Well," Ducky said, "my parents named me after Marian Anderson. I'm sure you've heard about her. She was a concert singer a long time ago. My dad heard her sing when he was a boy, and he never forgot it."

"I loved reading about her," Carlie said. "She was a very courageous lady. She was the first black person to sing at the Metropolitan Opera in New York."

Ducky smiled in the darkness. "I don't want anybody to know that's my real name until I've accomplished enough to be worthy of using it. Then I'll chuck 'Ducky' and be Marian Anderson Dumont."

The Bee Theres stood close together there in the flower-scented night under the old pine tree.

Sunshine knew she'd remember this day all her life. It had been full of lows and highs. Maybe the highest point of all was realizing how glad she was that Ducky had been patched into their lives.

She was glad too that she hadn't already picked a new name. She would do it later, after she'd accomplished something really great. Maybe she'd be Fleuretta, the great fashion designer. Or maybe she'd take the name Helen, after her favorite teacher. Or maybe she'd be Mrs. Arvy Dixon. Who could tell?

In the meantime she'd just enjoy being Sunshine. Everybody needed a little Sunshine in their lives, didn't they?

About the Author

When Lael Littke was a Beehive girl in Mink Creek, Idaho, she loved to ride her horse and dream of someday living in a big city where she would be a writer. Now that she lives in Pasadena, California, and has written and published more than two dozen books, she loves to remember those wonderful days when she was young. She enjoys associating with the young people of her ward in Pasadena, California, and relies on them for ideas for her books. She has one daughter and a houseful of dogs and cats.

BOOKS BY LAEL LITTKE

From Deseret Book

The Bee There Series
1. *Getting Rid of Rhoda*
2. *The Mystery of Ruby's Ghost*
3. *Star of the Show*
4. *There's a Snake at Girls Camp*

Where the Creeks Meet

From Other Publishers

Tell Me When I Can Go
Trish for President
Shanny on Her Own
Loydene in Love
Prom Dress
Blue Skye
The Watcher
The Peanut Butter Pond Series (6 books)
The Tall Tale Series (6 books)